MOBILE LEARNING MINDSET

THE IT PROFESSIONAL'S GUIDE TO IMPLEMENTATION

CARL HOOKER

International Society for Technology in Education
PORTLAND, OREGON • ARLINGTON, VIRGINIA

Mobile Learning Mindset
The IT Professional's Guide to Implementation
Carl Hooker

© 2017 International Society for Technology in Education
World rights reserved. No part of this book may be reproduced or transmitted in any form or by any means—electronic, mechanical, photocopying, recording, or by any information storage or retrieval system—without prior written permission from the publisher. Contact Permissions Editor: iste.org/about/permissions-and-reprints; permissions@iste.org; fax: 1.541.302.3780.

Editor: *Emily Reed*
Copy Editor: *Kristin Landon*
Cover Design: *Brianne Beigh*
Book Design and Production: *Kim McGovern*

Library of Congress Cataloging-in-Publication Data available.

First Edition
ISBN: 978-1-56484-397-5
Ebook version available

Printed in the United States of America

ISTE® is a registered trademark of the International Society for Technology in Education.

About ISTE

The International Society for Technology in Education (ISTE) is the premier nonprofit organization serving educators and education leaders committed to empowering connected learners in a connected world. ISTE serves more than 100,000 education stakeholders throughout the world.

ISTE's innovative offerings include the ISTE Conference & Expo, one of the biggest, most comprehensive ed tech events in the world—as well as the widely adopted ISTE Standards for learning, teaching and leading in the digital age and a robust suite of professional learning resources, including webinars, online courses, consulting services for schools and districts, books, and peer-reviewed journals and publications. Visit iste.org to learn more.

Also by Carl Hooker

Mobile Learning Mindset: The District Leader's Guide to Implementation

Mobile Learning Mindset: The Principal's Guide to Implementation

Mobile Learning Mindset: The Coach's Guide to Implementation

Mobile Learning Mindset: The Teacher's Guide to Implementation

Mobile Learning Mindset: The Parent's Guide to Supporting Digital Age Learners

To see all books available from ISTE, please visit iste.org/resources.

About the Author

 **Carl Hooker** has been involved in education since graduating from the University of Texas in 1998. He has been in a variety of positions in both Austin Independent School District (ISD) and Eanes ISD, from first grade teacher to virtualization coordinator.

Hooker is now director of innovation and digital learning at Eanes ISD. He is also the founder of the learning festival iPadpalooza (http://ipadpalooza.com). As director, he uses his background in both education and technology to bring a unique vision to the district and its programs. During his tenure, Eanes has jumped into social media, adopted the Google Apps for Education, and started to build a paperless environment with Google Docs. Hooker helped spearhead the Learning and Engaging through Access and Personalization (LEAP) program, which put 1:1 iPads into the hands of all K–12 students at Eanes.

Hooker has been a part of a strong educational shift toward technology integration. From his start as a teacher to his current district technology leadership role, he has always held one belief: Students need to drive their own learning. He realizes the challenges in our current public educational institutions and meets them head-on. His unique blend of educational background, technical expertise, and humor makes him a successful driving force for this change. Hooker also works as a keynote speaker and consultant through his company HookerTech, LLC.

Contents

Contents

CHAPTER 5
KEYS TO A HAPPY MARRIAGE OF IT AND CURRICULUM

CHAPTER 6
BUILDING AND SUPPORTING THE BACKBONE

CHAPTER 7
POLICIES AND PROCEDURES

Preface

In January 2010, Steve Jobs took the stage at a major Apple event to announce the creation of a device that was in between a laptop and a smartphone. When he announced the iPad, the reviews were mixed. Wasn't this something that had been tried before, even with Apple's MessagePad? (http://en.wikipedia.org/wiki/MessagePad) How was this going to work in mainstream society when it was bigger and bulkier than a phone and didn't have the keyboard of a laptop?

At the time of the announcement, I was a virtualization coordinator for the district. The technology director (my boss at the time) looked at me with wonder when I showed my excitement over this announcement. "This is going to change the face of education," I told him. His response: "I bet they don't sell even a million of them. It's like a crappy version of a laptop, only you can only do one thing at a time on it. It doesn't even have a USB port!"

In retrospect, I should have taken that bet, as Apple went on to sell a million in pre-orders alone. Flash forward a few more months. On April 2nd I was promoted to the role of Director of Instructional Technology. The very next day the first-generation iPad began to be sold in U.S. stores. I point this all out to show that even with all the prep work and sweat necessary for a successful device deployment, some synergy is also required.

As Director of Instructional Technology, I was taking over a dying role of sorts. Many districts were cutting the position at that time in Texas, and some felt it was a "nice to have" more than "a need to have" position. Knowing that going in, I made it one of my personal missions to erase the thought from the minds of the purse-string holders that my position could ever become obsolete. In fact, I set out to do the exact opposite: make them think they couldn't function successfully without it.

A big part of any leadership position is assessing risks. With the announcement of the iPad, my mind immediately went to education. How could these devices help students personalize their own learning? How would they enhance engagement and the learning experience of students? Are those gains in engagement and personalization enough to justify giving every student one of these devices?

These questions and many others went through my mind and those of many of the leaders in my district in the months that followed. Ultimately, in the fall of 2010, our district took the first steps toward providing 1:1 mobile devices. Whereas some districts chose to make big splashes with their first deployment, our initiative started with a forward-thinking librarian (Carolyn Foote) purchasing six first-generation iPads for students and teachers to check out.

Enter the second synergistic event. A group of leaders including myself made a trip to Cupertino, California, for an executive briefing on Apple's ideas for iPads in education. Before lunch of the first day, the Westlake High School principal leaned over and said to us, "We need one of these for every student." At that time, iPads were considered purely consumptive devices—a nice way to read a book or take notes, but nothing in the way of creativity. That trip to Apple's headquarters changed all of that for those in the room, even those who had been skeptical.

When we returned, we went on to expand the pilot to around 70 different users. From special education students to principals to high school AP teachers, we had as many key stakeholders as possible get their hands on this device to put it through its paces. At this point the iPad 2 had just launched and had a lot more functionality for creativity than its predecessor, namely the addition of a camera.

The pilot went on to expand into Westlake High School the following fall, and eventually reached all 8,000 Eanes ISD K–12 students by the spring of 2013. Here's an early blog post right after launch of the pilot on the EanesWifi site: http://eaneswifi.blogspot.com/2011/09/wifi-pilot-gets-started.html. Along the way, we've seen the highs and lows of having a device for every student, especially one as nimble and easy to use as an iPad.

The Mobile Learning Mindset series chronicles that journey from the perspective of six different components. Each component was key to making the initiative as successful as it's become, and as you'll learn, they are all intertwined with each other. This series is not specifically geared toward a 1:1 or Bring Your Own Device (BYOD) initiative. It's meant to be read as a handbook for any teacher, leader, or parent who is involved with a school that is using mobile device technology in the classroom.

The first book goes into detail about what district leadership can and should do to make a mobile device initiative successful. Having a strong, clearly defined goal and vision for a district that's well communicated is an important part of the process. From the superintendent to the school board to the district- and campus-level administrators, all need to be singing the same lyrics in the song of 1:1, or else it may fall flat.

The second book in the series is specifically focused on campus leaders and how they can support and showcase the initiative at the campus level. The book discusses the role the campus leader plays in terms of parent communication, teacher expectations, and highlighting student-led projects in the classroom.

The third book in the series focuses on diving into ideas and best practices for professional development around 1:1. I've seen many a district, including my own, continue the previous practices of professional development of a "sit 'n' get" style of learning, all the while preaching about how the students need to be the center of the learning. This book focuses on how to make that shift in your organization and ideas on how to make learning more engaging for your staff.

The fourth book offers an in-depth look at how mobile devices affect the classroom and what teachers can do both right out of the box and farther down the road to sustain a successful student-led learning environment. Using mobile devices just as a substitute for a textbook is a waste of money. These devices are multimedia studios of creation, but often that use is restricted by the classroom teacher. Book 4 explores models such as SAMR and tools that a teacher can use right away to shift the way learning takes place from a traditional classroom to a mobile classroom.

The fifth book is intended for parents, who must be informed and educated on the ins and outs of having mobile devices around the home. Part of the disruptive effect that mobile devices have on learning also affects the home. Parents are now facing dilemmas of social media, cyberbullying, and digital footprints that their parents never had to deal with.

None of this is possible without proper technical support. From infrastructure to break-fix scenarios, having a technology services department on board is vital. This book, the last in the series, is centered around that support. Technology changes so frequently that it is nearly impossible to create a book that has all the latest trends and gadgets. This book focuses on some necessary components of supporting a 1:1 mobile device initiative, as well as how to work with leaders, teachers, trainers, and parents on making the initiative a success.

Each book has a similar structure. Included among the chapters is one on "top 10 things not to do," an interview with an area expert in that book's particular focus, and chapters dedicated to ideas and strategies for interacting with all the other "players" in a mobile device initiative. In other words, how does a district leader support his/her teachers in this new environment? What expectations should the campus administrator have for his/her staff in terms of professional development? And conversely, how can professional development support those expectations?

All six of these components are parts of the very complex, constantly evolving machine that is a mobile learning initiative. Each plays its part, and each requires different amounts of attention and support from the other parts in order to work efficiently. Neglecting one of these components will result in the other parts having to work harder and could ultimately cause the machine to break down. My hope is that if you use this book series to learn how all the parts work, your own mobile learning machine will be a thing of beauty for your students. After all, their learning and their future is the ultimate reason to do something as bold as an initiative using mobile devices in the classroom.

Good luck, and thank you for being a part of this mobile learning revolution!

—*Carl Hooker*

INTRODUCTION

"I can't teach today, my projector is dead."

It's amazing to think how quickly we've gone from techno-phobia to techno-dependence. When I was teaching at the turn of the century, integrating technology meant having a few desktop computers in the back of the room that kids could work on. The only mobile devices we had were those greenish-looking word processors called AlphaSmart.

There was one projector in the building, and it was the size of a small aircraft carrier. When I brought it into my class to use it, I had to make sure kids weren't sitting next to it because it put out as much heat as a 1000-degree pizza oven. Most of the time, teachers' technology use was limited to the tried-and-true overhead projector (I used to hate coming home with "purple marker bruise" on the side of my hand).

That was only about 12 years ago, which makes the opening quote (actually said to me by a teacher in the last year) so impactful and remarkable. Much of this is a direct reflection of society and the rapid influx of mobile devices into our world. What we see as "needs" has changed almost overnight. In fact, I've seen several different versions of the "New Maslow's Hierarchy of Needs" making the rounds on the internet. Those 21st-century needs now include stellar Wi-Fi and long battery life before even considering food and shelter (see Figure 0.1).

To a person whose job it is to support this influx of technology and devices in schools, the task may seem daunting. So many more moving parts means many more new systems to monitor, support, and learn.

Before we embarked on our mobile learning journey, I was working in the technology services department as a virtualization coordinator. Although my background was in education, it was great to learn how systems, servers, and networks all work together. Anyone who works in a technology department knows that when the phone rings, it's usually not someone calling to tell you how great the Wi-Fi is running. Putting out fires is a 24/7 job even without handing every student a device—so how do you not only support a mobile learning initiative, but also help make it thrive?

Having a shared vision is a big part of that. This book series is designed to give all stakeholders a voice and common vocabulary when it comes to leading a mobile device initiative. Because technology changes rapidly, this book won't focus on a particular hardware or software solution but instead tackle the issues that arise whenever you're putting learning in the hands of kids in the form of a device.

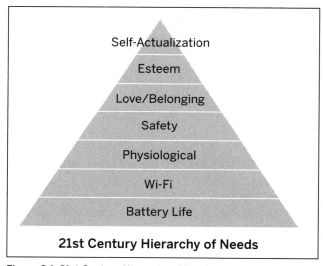

Figure 0.1 21st Century Hierarchy of Needs.

How to Use This Book

This book is broken down into various chapters that serve as both a guide and a resource for technology departments, depending on the state of your mobile learning initiative. The structure of the chapters in this book mirrors the structure of the other books in the series, though the content differs. Although the intended audience is technology directors or Chief Technology Officers in a mobile device initiative, teachers, parents, and administrators can also gain some insights into the role that IT plays during this process. No single department can support a mobile learning initiative alone—it takes the entire team.

The first five books really tackle both the "why" and "how" of mobile learning. Getting leadership on board with encouraging a learning culture and having professional learning that supports the teacher is key. This book is all about the "what" when it comes to supporting a mobile learning initiative from the IT side.

In the first chapter we'll really tackle getting the right mindset around a mobile device initiative and "agreeing to the why." Part of this is realizing that schools are not truly enterprise systems, as many would assume. Individualizing learning means individualizing the technology needs of each student. The role of IT is to figure out how to effectively support that individualization without creating too many roadblocks.

In Chapter 2, as is my custom with every book in the series, I'll tackle the top 10 things *not* to do in a mobile device initiative from the IT side. From *not* working in isolation to *not* rolling out everything all at once, many of these are common mistakes that we can still fall prey to from time to time.

Chapter 3 is an interview with an industry expert. As I explain in my introduction to CIO Leo Brehm, he is the rare person who, when you talk with him, within five minutes you'll have some new, creative idea on how to improve learning with technology. In his interview we talk about the ever-changing role of the IT leader and why education is bad when it comes to creating data silos.

Chapters 4 and 5 really focus on the communication and "marriage" of IT with curriculum and instruction. Both of these chapters provide examples of techniques we've used in our district to improve the relationship between departments, and also how to create a transparent communication path between IT and teaching staff when systems are changing.

Because technology is always changing, I spend quite a bit of time in Chapters 6 and 7 talking about some general structures and policies to have in place to support a mobile device initiative. I list some examples of companies we use for our Mobile Device Management (MDM) and also repairs, but know that these can change based on your device choice, district location, and size of implementation.

Chapter 8 is really all about finding out what is the best "Return on Learning" (R.O.L.) for the systems and digital resources you have in place. Districts have dived into the mobile device world with a focus on the hardware, when in reality there are thousands of dollars spent on software and applications that largely go unchecked. This chapter really talks about how to best process all these data points and turn that information into action to improve systems and learning.

In our final two chapters, I tie together the other components of this book series and how the IT department interacts with all those other components when successfully supporting a mobile learning initiative. Having open communication—from campus administrator to teacher to parent—can help avoid any surprises or frustrated stakeholders along the way. Taking time to gather feedback and reflect can go a long way in making your department an unstoppable force in the support of learning with technology.

"Easter Eggs"

According to Wikipedia (mrhook.it/easter), an Easter egg is "an inside joke, hidden message, or feature in an interactive work such as a computer program, video game or DVD menu screen." Why can't we also have these in books? In this book, I've hidden several Easter eggs that you'll have to uncover and discover. Some are buried in words, others in images. How do you reveal them? If you are reading this book in its paper form, you'll need to download the Aurasma app (www.aurasma.com/#/whats-your-aura) and find the trigger images to unlock the Easter eggs. Find and follow the "MLM Vision" channel to make it all work. Instructions can be found here: mrhook.it/eggs. Happy hunting!

CHAPTER 1

AGREEING TO THE "WHY"

Technology departments have grown in so many industries, both in and out of education, over the years. Early permutations helped fix copy machines and televisions; the latest versions support everything from wireless signal strength to augmented reality.

When a district embarks on a 1:1 or BYOD initiative, it is really saying there is a shared belief that the use of technology in schools is a good thing. One of my favorite resources for having a shared belief is Simon Sinek's TED Talk on "How Great Leaders Inspire Action" (mrhook.it/sinek).

In the talk, Simon discusses a clear difference in marketing between some pretty big-name technology companies and the focus of their efforts. One of the companies he praises is Apple and their ability to focus on the "Why" during their advertising more than the "What." You'll see people exploring a reef, or hang-gliding, or flying a plane with their devices in hand. You won't see device specifics, storage information, or RAM data. Other companies have obviously seen this strategy and its success, because they've run with it as well, focusing on the story more than the product.

In schools, it's much the same. We need to focus on the "Why" more than the "What," but regularly that doesn't happen. We spend hours discussing which device is right for our students instead of looking at why and how we want kids to have an immersive learning experience. Technology departments most directly deal with the "What" in those decisions, but being on the same page as the district vision and "agreeing to the why" goes a long way toward the success of a program.

We Are Not an Enterprise

During my time in IT, I would often be approached by companies telling me about their enterprise solutions for our district. Although I agree that maintaining thousands of devices and systems in a business makes it sound as if we are an "enterprise," I would argue in many ways we are not.

When I think of companies that use technology as an enterprise system, I see an old or dying model that has the exact same computer in every cubicle, each running the exact same software. Although I'm not saying that some form of standardization is a bad thing for support and training, the education space is no longer a one-size-fits-all system, as it was when technology first started to be introduced.

In an effort to personalize learning for students, we have to differentiate the devices based on the learning outcome, not the support need. From that aspect, I'd argue that we are no longer a "standard enterprise" when it comes to technology needs. An IT department that is built on the standard enterprise model will quickly struggle with the rapid pace of change and challenges presented during a mobile learning initiative. Instead, you need to focus on those systems that you can standardize and optimize, such as wireless access points and network infrastructure. As more and more applications move to the web with HTML5-responsive design, the devices will eventually not matter.

Marriage Counseling

In my years of working on "both sides of the house," I have seen several districts, including my own, struggle with the marriage between IT and instruction. In my current role, dealing with both curriculum and instruction as well as the technology services department, I sometimes think my title should be "Digital Marriage Counselor." I actually think this relationship is so vital to a successful initiative that I dedicate most of Chapter 5 to discussing this relationship and the pitfalls to avoid.

Purchases, like digital textbooks, are made with thousands of dollars invested by curriculum and instruction, but often without input or oversight from the department that will ultimately be supporting it. On the flip side, sometimes technology departments can purchase equipment or create images for machines that actually hinder learning or access to learning technologies.

In both of these situations, nothing is done maliciously or thoughtlessly. In many cases, these situations can be avoided with proper communication, but often that only happens after the fact. Both sides of the marriage get upset because they don't feel they are listened to or understood. As hard as it might seem sometimes, remember that the role of a technology department in a school district is ultimately to support learning. That does not necessarily mean saying "yes" to everything that curriculum and instruction asks for, but it does mean working with them to figure out the best solution for all involved.

Clearing Roadblocks to Learning

One of the biggest challenges in the current environment is that there are now a multitude of devices, browsers, digital resources, and apps that are a part of the learning process. Supporting learning even less than a decade ago meant making sure the projector worked and that the computer lab was up and running by the first week of school.

In my current environment, we support 14,000 devices for 9,000 students and staff. That includes iPads, laptops (both PC and Mac), desktops, projectors, printers, and audio systems. We also now have 32 different digital subscriptions that we either pay for or support. Combining all of these variables with a small crew of staff means that you have to automate and optimize whenever possible. Luckily, much of the back-end technology that comes with running active directory authentication and mobile device management (MDM) allows for much of this to be run with one or two staff members.

At the end of the day, your job is to not only support the learning, but also to clear roadblocks with technology that could inhibit students' ability to access the systems that will help them with learning. As long as that is your department mantra, you will find the work both challenging and rewarding as you support your district's mobile device initiative.

CHAPTER 2

TOP 10 THINGS NOT TO DO

Over the years, I've accrued more than my fair share of examples of what not to do in a mobile device initiative. From the classroom to leadership, this top 10 list appears in each and every book. This list is focused on the IT support side and includes some painful lessons that I hope your department can learn from.

1. Do *Not* Forget to Count

This may seem like an easy and obvious problem to avoid, but I think it bears mentioning. Managing multiple devices, whether in a 1:1 situation or not, means that you have to account for everything that goes out and in with staff and students. We distribute technology to staff on the first day of new-teacher orientation and pick it up from them on the day they resign, retire, or quit. Keeping track of all of this technology without a lot of support can be a major challenge and potentially cost your district thousands of dollars if you don't have a strong inventory system.

Even when you do have an effective inventory system in place, you may still be caught off guard. Whether it's a slew of last-minute hires, or a few extra students enrolling, there may be a time when you turn to distribute a piece of technology and realize that you don't have the inventory. What follows is a true story, albeit somewhat embarrassing, about what happened during our second year of 1:1 iPads.

On the second of our high school distribution days, we had pretty much accounted for everything, or so we thought. We changed the way distribution took place, centralizing it rather than going room to room, which was a great timesaver. However, in the course of handing kids back their iPads from the year before, rental iPads, or new iPads, our student count got lost in the shuffle. An order was placed (not naming names here) for what was thought to be the right amount, but in the end, it was about 200 devices short. As incredibly embarrassing as this is to share, it shows you that every minor detail can become major if not accounted for. I captured a video (visit mrhook.it/short to watch) of our assistant principal telling the last class period of students that we had run out. Not a great moment, but on the bright side we had some put aside for elementary. With a little extra effort, we were able to repurpose those in a few days for the kids without devices. Lesson learned, though: Always triple-check your counts and allow for a few extras.

2. Do *Not* Roll Out Everything at Once

Because of the timing of our bond package and when funds could became available, we didn't actually have iPads in hand and branded until mid-July. That meant we had to distribute the devices to staff and students all at once and during the first week of school. Many teachers only got to have the iPads in their hands for one month or less before school started. Not ideal when trying to make your staff comfortable with a new device. In a perfect world, they would have had them a year to a semester ahead of time. Or at least before the summer started.

Also, doing a massive deployment of more than 2,000 devices without testing it in a pilot environment meant that any challenges that arose were now multiplied to a much larger scale. Forget to put a certain permission on the devices? Now you have to go back and fix all of those mistakes by hand. Luckily, as I mentioned before, much of this is now manageable on the fly and can be reconfigured with the push of a button. That said, testing your rollout with a small subset of students or staff is advisable.

This is also true when it comes to pushing out new applications. We learned this lesson the hard way in our first year of 1:1. In our system, where the end user gets the apps, you don't want to force-feed all your apps down on the same day. This is especially true with larger apps, as we found out with the app GarageBand. The first year, we pushed this app out to students on the first day and by 10 a.m. the first morning, our entire mobile device management (MDM) server was crashing hard. Just as with rolling out hardware, pushing out all your software on the same day is not a great idea. The following year, we narrowed down our list of essential apps for day one and left off any apps that would take a heavy load on our servers until the weekend, when kids could download them using their own bandwidth at home. This spreads the downloads out over time so you don't have 1,500 kids downloading a 1.7-GB app during third period.

3. Do *Not* Take Away All Other Technology without Explanation

Getting rid of the old to replace it with the new is something every technology department spends the summer doing. However, I would never recommend taking the old (desktops in the backs of classrooms) and then waiting a few months before you put in the new (1:1 iPads in our case). Although it will increase appreciation for technology, it's not necessary and adds stress to the beginning of the year. You want them thirsty, but not at the expense of crossing the desert to get water (Figure 2.1). Consider a transition time when both are in the classroom, and remove the "old" only after the "new" is in.

Before our district moved toward becoming a Google Apps for Education school, we were using Novell GroupWise as our district's email system. Switching systems meant a lot of up-front training, but also a lot of warning as to when the system would change. Working with curriculum and instruction over the summer, we determined that a particular day in June would work best when making the change with staff.

Figure 2.1 Crossing the Technology Desert.

This presented a couple of challenges. One challenge was that staff would not be in the building during the transition. This meant that we couldn't be there to support them when the change was made. However, the bonus would be that they also wouldn't have to worry about learning and teaching, as most of the kids are out over the summer.

We prepared staff for the transition by sending out multiple communications before the end of school. We even started a countdown of sorts for the "Death of GroupWise." This was meant to sensationalize it somewhat, but it also caught the attention of staff who would normally dismiss any mass emails from the technology department. As we counted down the days leading up the transition, we didn't completely turn off GroupWise the day after the shift, either. We even sent an email to their GroupWise inbox at 11:59 p.m. before the transition telling them "ALERT! Your email is now on Google!"

Communicating the transition and leaving it open for a period of time helped us have a successful and seamless transition of a major communication platform for our district.

4. Do *Not* Work in Isolation

In order to collaborate and work with all departments, including curriculum and instruction, you cannot work in isolation. Districts that struggle with technology departments supporting their initiatives usually share two things: having a lack of communication and being physically disconnected.

Lack of Communication

I've mentioned it several times in this book, but communication, or lack thereof, tends to be the first place where support and collaboration break down. Departments make decisions that affect the entire district without discussion, dialogue, or discourse. Sometimes it is an honest oversight; other times it is done on purpose.

Physical Disconnection

Another issue that can cause a sense of isolation is when a technology department isn't visible in buildings and campuses. Many of the systems and break-fix issues can be done from a central hub to optimize personnel costs, but this also encourages departments to stay behind closed doors, giving almost a "person behind the curtain" feel to how they support staff and technology.

One way to improve on both of these issues is to get out and be visible and present on campuses. When I worked on creating a virtual desktop environment to extend the life of some of our desktop computers, I would create these virtual images with much input from people at the campus level. Then I would go and watch a computer lab full of students in action to see what issues might arise.

Did this take some of my time? Yes. Did I like everything I saw? No. But the staff at those campuses felt a level of support because I wasn't just a name behind an email or a voice on the other end of the line. I was actually there with them, helping their students through challenges and listening to their concerns. Although I couldn't fix every issue or concern they had, I did buy myself some credibility with them in creating this open line of communication and not isolating myself behind a screen.

5. Do *Not* Assume That Everyone Understands a Change

As mentioned in number 3, the transition to Google Apps for Education (GAFE) was one type of change where we communicated constantly and trained staff regularly to ease the transition. That said, the entire change to GAFE was nearly overturned because one person (the most important person in the district) did not understand the transition and the changes that happened to her email.

About 2 months after we had transitioned to Gmail as our mail client, I was called in to the superintendent's office. If you've read any of the other books in this series, you'll know that this superintendent was extremely supportive of technology integration and innovation. That said, the transition to Google was a struggle for her because she didn't understand why we changed from our previous system to this new system. At one point she even mentioned changing back the entire system because of her lack of comfort with it.

When I discussed with her some of the pros of making this transition, she listened to the reasons and understood them on a global scale, but was still struggling with the change. Further investigation revealed that she had a comfort with the older Novell GroupWise email client when it came to sorting and finding contacts. That's when I realized the difference between her and the rest of the staff, who hadn't struggled with the change—lack of training.

This made me acutely aware of two things. One is that when staff do not have or participate in training for a tool, they are immediately behind when it comes to using it and understanding its purpose. The other is that changing a system that's used by everyone means that each person who interacts with the system will have a different experience based on their own past experiences.

6. Do *Not* Be Afraid to Outsource from Time to Time

Managing people and budget on top of infrastructure, deployment, and service support can stretch the bandwidth of a department to the breaking point at times of high volume. In schools, summer months are held sacred as a time to catch up on some work orders and to do any major system changes. The problem that usually plagues schools is that when staff return at the beginning of the school year, those loose-end projects collide with start-of-the-year issues.

One side effect of a mobile learning initiative that I'll address in later chapters is the support of digital resources. When students are either issued a device or bring in their own, it adds a layer of complexity to your department that you didn't have to support beforehand. So you now you've added additional devices to support and more network to manage on top of digital resource deployment.

One thing that has helped our department over the years is outsourcing some of the low-hanging fruit (such as collecting old machines or wiring through ceiling tiles) to others. As these are generally menial tasks that don't present a sophisticated level of complexity, they don't necessarily cost thousands of dollars, either. One of the advantages of working in a school district is the abundance of students who are off for the summer and looking for some quick work and to develop some skills that may beef up their résumé for later in life. Why not tap those resources in a win-win scenario that frees up some time for harder and more complex projects?

There may be also be a time when paying for some automation of a task can save hundreds of worker hours on the back end. We have been struggling to onboard our digital textbooks and having to do many of the uploads of .csv files manually. The only problem is, the data changes almost daily with students changing classes. So this past year, rather than having someone spend hours each week managing that, we paid a programmer to code an automated solution where students log into one place and access the books they should have access to based on their enrollment.

7. Do *Not* Be Surprised When Students Try to Break Your Systems

Whether you are handing devices to every student or allowing them to bring their own (or both, in our case), there are always a couple of things that kids have that adults don't have. One is the gift of time and the other is a lack of responsibility. Although these gifts can be seen as avenues toward following creative pursuits, they also allow students to test boundaries and get into mischief.

A couple of years ago, a middle school student approached us and said that he could break into our grade-book system fairly easily. (Think Matthew

Broderick from *War Games,* only without the threat of global warfare.) We were concerned, but also happy that he approached us with the vulnerability concern. The question became, what to do? Punish this kid?

We decided instead to put him to work. We asked him to actually hack our system and come up with a vulnerability report. He had a time frame in which he could do it, and then he had to publish all of his findings to us in a professional matter. In return, not only would he not be in trouble, but we would give him a commendation to add to his portfolio for later in life when he would surely become a white hat hacker.

Kids love the creative challenge of finding flaws in your systems. The key isn't being fearful of that, but instead figuring out creative ways to put that curiosity to good use.

8. Do *Not* Forget Who Your Customers Are

For someone working daily in a technology department, it's easy to get lost in the wires and boxes of technology (see number 4). During my time in the technology department, I became dismayed and negative when certain "problem teachers" would call. Many times the problems were user-related, so this added to the frustration. I started to dread hearing the phone ring.

I'm not sure when it happened exactly, but I became the very person that I hated. We work in a people business. Our product is student learning, and everything we do should be geared toward that outcome. Sometimes in the middle of this technology revolution, IT staff will lose focus on this objective. They will become jaded and have to fight the urge to roll their eyes when a phone rings. We must never lose sight of who our customers are in this business. It's the teachers and students doing the most vital work to make sure the technology we put into their hands actually helps with learning.

So the next time the phone rings from that same teacher who has called many times before, remember that they are calling not to bother you, but to ensure that technology is working to support the learning experience for their students.

9. Do *Not* Let Your Personal Philosophy Drown Out the Community

Over the years during this mobile learning revolution, there have been many different devices and many different ways to support them. Within the 1:1 device world alone, there are options that range from high-end laptops to Google's Chromebook to Apple's iPad. All of these models come with a variety of philosophies when it comes to control and support.

The beauty and educational relevance of these devices is the personalization of learning that can happen. I have felt for a number of years that this becomes null and void the second you turn this into just another "system" to manage through your technology department. Although some levels of control, such as age restrictions and filters, are appropriate for certain ages, remember that you are trying to teach these students some self-control as well. Not every system can be controlled and managed. That said, you must find the happy medium between control and learning.

My personal philosophy of openness with the devices and the App Store was challenged when we started the process to refresh our devices. Many of the teachers, students, and community members mentioned the seemingly insurmountable distraction of having the entire App Store open on devices, even with an age restriction. It seemed that many had decided that even using the devices posed a risk that there would be extreme off-task behavior and a lack of self-control from students in and out of the classroom. So, in the fall of 2016, it was decided that we would remove the App Store from the devices and instead populate the devices with our own version of an app store, where we decide what goes in and what doesn't.

Being philosophically opposed to this presented a problem, but I was also not going to be so self-centered that I ignored the cries for help from my customers. To find that happy medium, we decided to implement the "no app store" approach but also allow teachers and students to submit requests for apps to be added. The outcome has been tremendous. The devices are being used for much more meaningful instructional reasons, and the fear and fight over off-task behavior has dwindled. Control with a mix of some level of personalization can be good. It's a tenuous balance that all districts must face during their mobile learning initiatives.

10. Do *Not* Let Fear Deter You from Your Mission or Vision

"Every challenge presents an opportunity."

I was told that early on in my career, and it has always stuck with me. There will be times when you're attempting something new that will give you and those in the district fear. This fear of change is a natural and instinctive part of our existence as humans. It's that same fear that kept us from burning ourselves up when we first discovered fire. In general, humans all carry a sense of fear when it comes to the unknown—meaning change.

Whatever the reason for the fear, it should not deter you from moving forward on your initiative. Instead, use it to guide you and alert you to possible issues that might arise and opportunities that will come up because of this change. The vision is always the goal. When you make decisions about your program, let that be your guide—not fear.

CHAPTER 3

INTERVIEW WITH LEO BREHM

I've enjoyed this chapter in each of the six books I've written. Getting a variety of perspectives on successes and failures in mobile learning can help guide your program going forward. In this chapter, I interview Leo Brehm (@leobrehm), CIO of Northborough-Southborough Public School District in Massachusetts. I've enjoyed getting to know Leo over the years, and he's one of the first people I go to whenever I have a problem or idea in the area of educational technology. In this candid interview, we discuss everything from the changes he's seen with technology in education to why he thinks it would be cool to have a "Point of View" gun like the one from *A Hitchhiker's Guide to the Galaxy*.

Leo Brehm

I've appreciated Leo's thoughts on educational technology throughout the years and even unearthed a quote about technology and content that I plan to steal (with credit!) in my future presentations about textbooks and learning. As with all my interviews, the link to the video version of the interview is at the end of this chapter. Because we were both in remote locations, you'll only see icons of our heads, but if you want to hear the unedited version, it's worth a listen.

Carl Hooker: I'm excited today to invite a good friend of mine, Leo Brehm to this series. There are some people I go to for inspiration. There are some people I go to learn things. Leo is neither of those.

Leo Brehm: *(Laughs)*

CH: However, Leo is one of the very few people in the world that I can talk to on the phone and within 5 minutes have some sort of crazy, creative idea (some of which are good, others of which are not so good). So I'm honored to have him be a part of this interview. This book is all about IT staff, and I know that Leo has done time in that department for several years in several different districts. So let's start with that. First of all, thanks for joining us.

LB: Happy to be here.

CH: Tell me a little bit about yourself, and then tell me your "origin" story and how you got started in all of this.

LB: My mother was a special education teacher who dealt with a lot of adaptive technology. When I was in grade school, she used to bring home Apple IIes and adaptive technology, and I got really into it at that point. One thing she told me, though, was "Don't go into education—go into business."

CH: *(Laughs)*

LB: *(Laughs)* And so if we flash forward to my college years—some people took a gap year; I decided to take a gap three years—when I went back, I decided that I couldn't just go to school full-time as I had gotten used to working full-time. So I decided to be a tech aide in the elementary school that I'd gone to. This whole experience happened in the 1995–96 timeframe, and I joined a district team to write curriculum for technology integration. The following year, I became the network administrator for the Sharon School District next door, in a small bedroom community outside of Boston. [Sharon] was very progressive in the ed tech space. I was fortunate enough to be there for a few years as the network admin and the only technician for a while. We had instructional tech specialists on hand. We were going through that evolution as many districts at the time were as business teachers to technology skill sets and what that meant and how to embed those into the regular curriculum.

When I finished up my undergrad degree, they asked me to teach high school and middle school part-time, which was wonderful. I was on waiver, of course, because I didn't have a teaching degree.

CH: Really? I didn't know that.

LB: Yeah, it took some time. Then my superintendent suggested that I go "legitimate," so I went for my master's in instructional technology, and during that timeframe I also became the director of IT at Sharon. It was a wonderful experience and opportunity.

In the early 2000s, as you know, it was just a vibrant time for tech and ed, or "edtech" as we call it now, and everything kind of snowballed from there. In 2007, I joined MassCUE (masscue.org) as a board member and quickly became the conference chair—which is a dubious honor because of the amount of work involved.

CH: I'm sure that's a high-paying gig.

LB: It was a great experience. We ended up moving our yearly conference to Gillette Stadium, home of the New England Patriots, and that really put MassCUE back on the map. We became the leader in the state when it came to integration of technology. We were able to partner with the Massachusetts superintendents' associations, and it was a great learning experience connecting what happens in the classroom with what's happening at the state level—the roles both play in making the integration of technology a success.

In 2011, I became the president of MassCUE and also the IT Director of Newton Public Schools, which is a small city outside of Boston and home to the Fig Newton. Some of us remember that cookie. It's probably full of white flour and calories and probably not a source of good food, but. ...

CH: Is it gluten-free?

LB: *(Laughs)* Yeah, exactly. So that's how I got to where I am now. I'm currently the CIO for a regional district in the middle of the state called Northborough-Southborough (nsboro.k12.ma.us) and doing some consulting. I'm happy to work with numerous school districts across the Commonwealth, which is exciting.

CH: Backing up to the mid-90s through today, that spans 20+ years, what would you say is the biggest change you've seen in schools with technology since you started in 1995? What's one thing you would consider a game changer?

LB: I think it's when technology went more mobile. That's where it went from something like a garnish to more of a mindset shift. Maybe back in the '09 or '08 timeframe, where people began to really think about how they integrate it. They used to create backup plans in case the tech didn't work, but that happened less and less. Tech became something they can trust. And mobilizing it allowed it to make its way into the classroom more quickly, out of the fixed or dedicated lab area, where you had to move the kids to it. Now the technology could go to them with much more ease. And then up to today where it's coming in with every student. It's become part of our culture. It's ubiquitous now. I just think that was one of the major shifts in ed tech that allowed teachers to take risks.

CH: I like that analogy of a garnish. Like instead of the icing on the cake, it's now baked into the cake.

LB: Right. It's because there is no more wow factor just because it's on a screen. I mean, curriculum on a screen 12 years ago had a wow factor. Now everything is on the screen, and it's expected. Our children are flipping magazines expecting the pages to move like iPads.

CH: So speaking of iPads, this book series is all about mobile learning—so what are some of the challenges that CTOs might face when implementing a mobile device initiative?

LB: I still think it's the curriculum. I think our system still has a strong mindset that we start on paper first. It's hard to break out of that mold because it's how we learned. The teachers of today and when you and I learned, everything was based on that textbook and a scope and sequence based on the page numbers.

CH: Right!

LB: Whereas today the book is "round," not flat. You don't have to go from one page to the next, you can now go to any "page," anywhere as needed. Teachers need to construct their lessons in that manner. Now lessons have to be more interactive and more multi-directional. It allows all that data to accumulate and allows teachers to peek at the learning of each student, though I don't think the teachers quite realize what is now possible as an attribute to having this technology.

CH: Yeah, it's interesting. For someone who's been in this at the early stages like you and me, most of the challenges were technical. Now that the expectation is there, the curriculum is really the thing that's holding it back. So for those of you reading this book, know that this is the technical side of it and there are expectations and challenges to overcome, but once you do that, there are additional challenges that come from the curricular side.

LB: I think the technical parts comes with the "know-how." It's one of the biggest gaps we saw in Newton where our infrastructure was second to none and we had the kind of access we wanted. We didn't quite call it "1:1," but essentially we were in the schools. It was challenging to get the curriculum teams to understand the power of the digital side and the way that it could be conducted in the space. The shift really needed to come from pedagogy to take advantage of the technology.

It's definitely light years ahead of where it was, but it's no longer about a stationary studio or Kid Pix where we used to truck the kids down to the lab to use it. Because there was a disconnect on which skills should be built. We used to call them "soft skills," but now we have standards that are built around the skills they need. That delta or gap of understanding between the teacher's perspective on just how they can meet those skill sets or standards within the history curriculum, science curriculum, math curriculum, and so on.

CH: Speaking of digital curriculum, one of the more hot topics today centers around student data privacy. Now that all this curriculum is digitized and students are logging in, where does all this information go? We're a G Suite for Education district, so we get some privacy questions from time to time. Where do you think this is all going in terms of education?

LB: It's something we have to face as a whole society—education is just a small part of that. It used to be something we had to worry about once we turned 18; now it's something we have to worry about the second we touch a digital device. Here in Boston, I was honored to take part in a consortium at Cambridge to come up with privacy policies for products and companies. It was written for several reasons—protecting the students' identity among the data while not hindering innovation that requires analyzing that usage data. I think we shouldn't be so quick to demonize the "profiteering" vendor. I would consider myself a sympathizer in ways, because not every company got into ed tech to make money quick. There aren't many billionaire ed tech vendors out there.

I think there needs to be a partnership with them to figure out how technology can truly reach its potential. Alan November published an article earlier this year talking about where ed tech failed and why it has failed. (Article here: mrhook.it/alan) I think we're partly to blame when we don't share insight and information.

CH: If we get too restrictive, then we aren't learning and sharing with each other. And I think you hit the nail on the head there about companies chasing the dollars. I mean, there's $9 billion in ed tech and hundreds of companies fighting for their slice of that.

LB: There's been some articles about IBM Watson's data product, and I often talk about the "Education Amazon Experience." Why can't the technology provide suggestions based on my preferences? And the reality about this, I was speaking recently with Michael Horne (Distinguished Fellow at the

Christensen Institute) about this, and we don't have enough data points. One thing about the data we do get, it's very disorganized. We don't have data governance to leverage the data appropriately, let alone leverage it to deliver a better product to us. It's a bit of a double-edged sword.

CH: Changing pace a little here, let me ask you this. Where do you go for inspiration? What inspires you?

LB: You mean aside from the recent series of books called *Mobile Learning Mindset?*

CH: *(Laughs)* You are allowed to stay in the interview now.

LB: *(Laughs)* For me, the most powerful part of working in technology the last eight or nine years is the professional network. The power of the network just recently helped me relocate careers when I was looking for a shorter commute to be with family. I've seen it with teachers to help improve their practice and to bounce ideas off of each other. The personal network we've built around us in ed tech enables us to find inspiration in what other people are doing. To be able to take that and twist it and make it fit our own environment.

Aside from that I read a lot of the industry publications like *Tech & Learning* (techlearning.com), but a lot of it really comes from conversations I have with my peers and my professional network. I also turn to a lot of innovation and cutting-edge technology. I really enjoy trying to figure out how cutting-edge technology can personalize and deepen the learning experience for kids. That's one of the great things about working in this industry—it's kind of our job to play with toys.

CH: I tell people that all the time. It's my job to look and play with this stuff, then I tell them whether it's good or not.

LB: Exactly! And how can we use it effectively? Recently I've been working on a product with FableVision (fablevision.com) out of Boston with Peter and Paul Reynolds on a K–12 technology application centered around animation. They have a K–8 platform that moves right into 9–12 with a professional application that used to be called Toon Boom. They've connected those animations and integrated them right into the core curriculum. I think it just provides an awesome opportunity for a percentage of our learners and how they can express themselves or make their thinking visible.

Sure, it also uses technology, but I think that's part of our new role. The term technology often boxes us into what we do every day, but in reality it's what the technology empowers that now drives what we do within our industry.

CH: What's something you've seen recently that really has you excited? That FableVision product sounds pretty cool, but is there anything else you have seen that has you excited when it comes to technology in education?

LB: Yes, that and the new open-source virtual reality platform being brought to STEAM. I've been working on setting up a lab for it, to create immersive learning experiences. Maybe set up an instance of something like Google's Tilt Brush (tiltbrush.com) which is a 3D painting and drawing environment where you put on a virtual reality headset and it lets you design all around yourself.

CH: Cool! I've never seen that in action, but I'm familiar with it.

LB: Yeah, we're excited about it. We want to incorporate it with FableVision and the work Peter Reynolds is doing. It's one of the ways we are going to get them onsite. The great thing is, those are no longer cost prohibitive. You know, for $2500 we can have a really high-tech setup that will really help that population in Western Massachusetts and a collaboration called "Central Mass Collaborative." We're taking an old bomb and tractor factory and our determination to turn it into a place of opportunity for a very diverse population in the greater Worcester area. So we're really excited about that collaboration between FableVision, Steelcase furniture, and SAFARI Montage to create these active learning spaces and classrooms. I really think to this population, it's going to make a world of difference.

CH: That's what it's all about. Creating those opportunities to stretch learning beyond their own community. Who would have thought five years ago we'd be able to put our phones in cardboard boxes and walk around looking at dinosaurs? It's crazy to think about.

LB: Exactly! It is. I'm excited to be someone that's helping deliver that experience. It's kind of the reason why we are all in it in a way. Creating those "aha" moments for all our teachers and our learners. Taking core concepts within our curriculum and technology can definitely help make those connections in ways we haven't even thought of yet.

CH: Think back to when you first got started in this role. What's a piece of advice you'd have for someone just getting started? What's something they should be wary of or keep their mind on?

LB: You know, they should do everything they can to understand the instructional space and what it's about. Far too often CIOs and CTOs come in from a pure IT prospective. You know, just "making it work" and far too restrictive or a "lockdown" mentality. I don't think it's as restrictive as it used to be, but you remember seven or eight years ago when many districts were blocking YouTube. I can't imagine that being viable today. I know back then that bandwidth was really an issue.

I think also the evolution of the school CIO—I think that it's much different from the traditional CIO. I think one thing I would give advice to someone starting out is that if you don't have a master's in education, you should at least take part in some core instructional courses of some kind. Then go and observe a few classrooms. Go see the technology in action and pay attention to the pain points and how can you remove those pain points and improve instruction in the classroom.

CH: There's a whole chapter in this book about the marriage of IT and C&I (Chapter 5), and I think you've totally led into that. The job has changed. It's not just about sitting behind the walls messing with wires anymore—everything is in the hands of your customers … the kids.

LB: One other thing I'd suggest is take a few courses on data infrastructure. One of the parts of supporting instruction these days is becoming more systemic. Beyond just the digital resources and content is the management of that content and the management of access to those resources. I'm sure at some point we'll talk about LMS (learning management systems) and the use of that word *management* can go in many directions. I think the primary use of it should be the management of content creation and delivery. I think instead of learning management it should be about learning experiences.

CH: Yes! An "LES" (learning experience system). Love that idea!

LB: Right. Creating a learning experience system. And it may not be just one single product. It may be easier if we can put everything in one basket, but we might also be limiting ourselves if we don't use best in breed within our industry. Maybe that's another piece of advice for a starting CIO—to be familiar with the data infrastructure and try to figure out how those data silos can talk to each other. I think trying to figure out how to create the best user experience will help advance your position within your learning community and your profession tremendously. Just having that conversation that this is the preferred user experience and this is what it's going to take to get there.

CH: We do have a lot of data, but we don't really do a good job of seeing it all and figuring out what is the complete package of a student when they leave our system because there are so many multiple data points. That's great advice for someone just entering the field.

Ok, time to change it up and go a little James Lipton style here. These are always interesting, just the first thing that pops into your head. Here we go. Word or sound that you hate to hear?

LB: The traditional school bell.

CH: Oh, you mean the actual school bell sound.

LB: Ding! Ding! Ding! Yes … it drives me crazy.

CH: What is something that gives you pride?

LB: Watching the "aha" moments and seeing kids connect the dots in a school that I'm working it. That gives me pride because I know that somehow, I'm a part of that system. And using technology is a part of that, but I'm proud of the work that I do in preparing the learners of tomorrow.

CH: That's awesome. I would say that's something I'm proud of too. So, name something that's really cool in your office.

LB: I have a pretty extensive set of the original Apple "Think Different" posters framed in my office.

CH: Ohhhh! Those are worth something!

LB: I like them a lot. When they first came out I got the set of 10 or 12 and there were certain people in my schools that liked different ones like people that were Beatles fans so I gave those out.

CH: I used to have the Muhammad Ali one somewhere.

LB: Yeah, that one is a rare one now. I have about 10 or 12 of them now but I've had to re-collect them. I think they are inspirational because they remind me of that speech that Richard Dreyfus did for Apple, the commercial? It reminds us of what our potential is.

CH: Here's to the crazy ones.

LB: That's it.

CH: Put a dent in the universe. That's what Steve (Jobs) said.

LB: Right.

CH: If you could have dinner with anyone in history, who would it be and why?

LB: That's a tough one because my initial thought would be Steve Jobs.

CH: Ok, let me rephrase that. If you could have dinner with anyone but not Steve, who would it be?

LB: A friend of mine actually had dinner with him once and said it was a very intense dinner, but that's a story for another time. You know, I would say Leonardo da Vinci.

CH: Going with your namesake there.

LB: The language gap might cause a problem, but it would be interesting [to hear] the questions he might ask me and how I might answer them.

CH: Well you definitely win for the oldest person in history of the people that I have asked. I don't think any one else has gone pre-1900s.

Ok, a couple more real quick. What's something that needs to be invented?

LB: The "Point of View" gun from *The Hitchhiker's Guide to the Galaxy.*

CH: Nice! What did that do?

LB: It wasn't in the book, it was made for the movie. But the concept came out of a book that was ghost-written by Douglas Adams. The concept was, if you had the gun and shot somebody, that person would immediately understand how you feel.

CH: Oh my gosh! We need that today!

LB: We do need that today. There is a bit of a gap of understanding. According to the book, it was developed by an association of disgruntled housewives who were at the point of their husbands just "not understanding how I feel." They could use the gun to make that happen.

CH: Here's the last fun one for you. When was the last time you sang, and what was the song?

LB: Yesterday. *(Laughs)*

CH: Oh! The song *Yesterday?* Or you sang yesterday?

LB: *(Laughs)* No I sang yesterday. I have music-loving children and my son has really gotten into that song *Paradise City* by Guns n' Roses. *(Laughs)*

CH: Nice! Did you do the whole Axl Rose thing and sway back and forth?

LB: No, I didn't perform it for him because I didn't want him to have to experience that.

CH: Yeah, I can see that. That's good though. You are bringing him up right teaching him the classics. *(Laughs)*

LB: *(Laughs)* Right. Well there's a good invention. Alexa (Amazon's Echo) allows my children to experience all different kinds of music just by asking.

CH: OK, last one. Any last piece of advice for anyone in IT who's about to lead a mobile device initiative?

LB: Make sure that every aspect of that initiative is meaningful. Don't just implement it for technology's sake. Always focus on the learning. Think about every aspect of the initiative for the teachers and the students and the parents. How will it empower learning? Both inside the classroom and anytime or anywhere?

CH: That is awesome. He is Leo Brehm ladies and gentlemen! You can follow him on Twitter at @leobrehm, and you can find him on LinkedIn as well. He is the CIO of Northborough-Southborough schools right there in Massachusetts. Thank you so much, Leo, for joining us today!

You can watch the full video interview with Leo here: mrhook.it/leo.
(*Note:* We were both in hard-to-reach places, so the video is a little choppy.)

CHAPTER 4

COMMUNICATION IS THE KEY TO EVERYTHING

"The second you feel like you are overcommunicating, double it."

A lot of married couples experience the following scenario. One of you wants to buy something and tries to tell your spouse about it by dropping hints. Rather than directly asking for it, you mention it when your spouse isn't paying attention, hoping to receive passive approval. Maybe they are watching their favorite reality TV show or their favorite sports team, so they nod and say "OK" without really giving it much thought. Eventually, though, something happens that alerts your spouse—say, they see the charge from the Amazon order, and they start to ask questions.

"Why didn't you tell me about this?"

Although technically you did tell your spouse about the purchase, they weren't really invested in the conversation until it affected them (or their budget). I feel like emails do much of the same thing. You can try to send out an alert from Technology Services about a service outage or an upcoming change, but realize that only about half the people you send it to will actually even open the email. As I mentioned in Chapter 2 about the 10 things *not* to do, when we attempted to switch our email system, we sent out multiple emails and still had people surprised when they woke up one morning and were no longer getting emails on the old system.

These days, we receive information from a variety of sources. This can be good and bad. It also means that as an organization trying to communicate with stakeholders, you are also competing with all of those other sources. Hoping that the one email in a stream of hundreds of emails may get read is only an initial step. Although email can handle small situations or clarifications, something as seismic as the shift in learning with mobile devices needs a variety of avenues of input and output.

Crowdsourcing Information

In the spring of 2015, our district passed a bond issue that included over $5 million for a line item called "Student Mobile Device Initiative." Even though we had a mobile device initiative in progress, we felt like this provided us with an opportunity to reboot and make adjustments. Not only that, but now we could reflect on the first few years of the program and gather input from a variety of sources. We knew the email and a few surveys wouldn't be enough. For a department supporting a mobile device initiative, the more information gathered, the better informed and prepared you can be when making tactical decisions.

Formation of a Digital Learning Task Force

With opportunity comes great responsibility. OK so maybe that wasn't the exact line from the Spiderman movie, but we knew that going forward, we needed to make sure that multiple voices were represented in choosing our next device. Rather than just form a "Technology Committee," we decided to create a "Digital Learning Task Force" (DLTF). The name was symbolic in that this was much more than just a selection of a device. The task force would be made up of teachers, students, parents, community members, and administrators.

In the summer, we publicly posted an application for members of the district community to apply to be a part of a newly formed task force that would ultimately recommend the final device. (Here's a copy of the application: http://mrhook.it/apply.) In September, we gathered some board members and administrators to look through the applications in an attempt to bring together a diverse group of parents from different schools in our community. We then did the same thing in choosing our teachers, students, and administrators to be a part of this team.

In our first meeting we discussed the two goals of this group:

1. Look at what our current reality is when it comes to integration of technology, and

2. Ask ourselves, what do we want our preferred future to be?

An additional part of this process and task force was trying to construct multiple ways not only to gather input from the district community but also to learn and investigate the current state of devices in schools. We decided that we would use six different avenues to communicate and gather input:

1. Digital learning symposiums

2. Feedback walls

3. Site visits

4. Focus groups

5. Online interactions

6. Surveys

Digital Learning Symposiums

In an effort to create more discussions around digital learning, we decided to host several symposiums open to the community as a launching point for these conversations. Each of these were captured via Livestream (livestream. com/eanesisd) for parents who couldn't make it in person or wanted to watch at a later date.

Each of the symposiums focused on a different component of the mobile device initiative and was intentionally laid out to address the areas where we struggled the most the first time around and let the task force hear all the concerns going forward.

The first one was an expert panel made up of industry experts, university professors, and people from the local start-up community. This group shared ideas of the future role of technology in the workplace and also identified trends and characteristics related to what companies wanted in their future employees. Although some of those desired traits included technology (such as coding or problem solving), much actually came back to the design of learning in the classroom. This was a great discussion for other leaders and curriculum members to hear, because focusing the discussion solely around technology isn't going to bring about improvements in learning.

The second panel was made up of a variety of teachers from across grade levels and disciplines and included some round-table discussions as well as the panel discussion. The round-table discussions were made up of a variety of teachers, and members of the task force and the community were encouraged to rotate from table to table asking questions and raising concerns. We placed note-takers at each table to capture the informal discussions taking place so that members of the DLTF could process what was said on their own time. During the panel discussion, we asked students to submit video questions to the staff as well. This added an element of collaboration and the voice of the students.

The final symposium was made up of students from first to 12th grade and also included some round-table discussions. Students are always refreshing to listen to, as they are usually the most honest and rough around the edges. This was certainly the case with our group. It was made up of a variety of students from different levels. From first to 12th grade, we heard the good, the bad, and the ugly of our previous initiative. Although this feedback could be hard to take at times, it did give us information we needed to improve going forward.

Feedback Walls

During the symposiums, we placed a series of feedback posters around the room and created online feedback walls using Padlet (padlet.com) to correlate with those around the room. The four posters asked the following questions (You can see the virtual walls by going to the links):

- What are some things we are doing well with technology? (tiny.cc/dltf1)

- What are some things that we need to improve? (tiny.cc/dltf2)

- What other things do we need to consider when it comes to tech? What's next? (tiny.cc/dltf3)

- What future ready skills do our students need? (tiny.cc/dltf4)

Site Visits

Some of the most powerful feedback can be gained by simply visiting a classroom. Often, the narrative in the community can be an exaggeration of what is actually taking place in the classroom. One of the first assumptions from the public community was that iPads were not really being used effectively in the K–2 classrooms. There was a feeling that we could provide laptops or higher-end devices to the high school students if we just took away the devices from the lower grades or went to a shared model. Before any decisions were made on that front, it was decided that the task force visit an elementary, middle, and high school campus first.

Through those visits, the task force saw in fact some of the most meaningful uses of the devices were happening at the lower levels of elementary. Even though those grade levels got access to those devices late in the program (some had only had them for 3 years), they actually had integrated them much more fully than even some of high school classes. It was through these site visits that another recommendation would come in that we need to do a better job of communicating what's happening in the classroom and which apps are being used districtwide.

Focus Groups

Because the symposiums were very public, it was sometimes difficult for people to share honestly what they were feeling or what concerns they had. As a result, the task force decided to host several focus groups for students, parents, and teachers at each of our campuses and even hosted a central one just for parents. These focus groups provided some great qualitative data as well. It's through the focus groups that we heard the most about the day-to-day issues with distraction and the need to occasionally have access to other devices when needed. These intimate interactions provide a non-threatening platform for people to share and give criticism and also feel more involved in the problem-solving process. We asked that members of these focus group come forward not only with problems, but also proposed ideas and solutions.

Online Interactions

As many on the task force mentioned, not everyone can get to a physical meeting or symposium. We all live busy lives, and given that this was all about digital learning it made sense to have an online component. So in addition to the symposiums being posted online and the interactive feedback posters shared via Padlet, we also created a Google Community. The community was a place where anyone could join and post questions or resources about digital learning. We also used the #EanesDLTF hashtag whenever information was shared or posted as a way to gather data. This hashtag would also be used as a way to curate questions for the panels at the symposium.

Survey, Survey, Then Survey Again

One of the final methods of data gathering was the use of surveys. Each survey focused on a different segment of our population and was focused on gathering information on both the current reality and our preferred future.

The results of the surveys were diverse and gave us a wide range of feedback. We saw a general tendency that the older the students were, the more they wanted to have a physical keyboard or laptop. Here's an example of some of the data we shared with the school board on that first survey (Figure 4.1).

As a result of this and a discrepancy at the high school in terms of what students and teachers preferred, we decided to send a follow-up survey once we had narrowed down the device choices. For many of the students and teachers

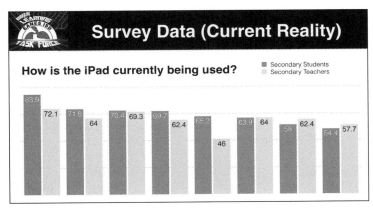

Figure 4.1 Sample data from our original DLTF student survey.

who preferred laptops, a high-end MacBook was their preferred machine of choice. The budget for the program wouldn't allow for a $1200 device, and because the uses they had outlined were so varied based on class, we needed to find a base-level device for all classes. We then took the final three devices (a MacBook, a Dell laptop, and an iPad Air 2 64GB with keyboard case) and made them available for viewing a week before sending the final high school survey. After students and staff had some time to physically look at the options and test them out, we sent follow-up surveys to get feedback and arrive at our final decision.

Communicating Our Final Recommendation

One thing was certain: no matter what we chose, some groups would be happy and some upset with the choice. After 600 hours of focus groups, discussions, meetings, presentations, and symposiums—as well as more that 6,000 survey responses—the task force voted unanimously for the option that gave us the most flexibility, with the best support model as well as ease of integration. In choosing the iPad Air 2 (64GB) for all levels, we were giving students and staff a model of iPad that was 12 times faster, held four times as much memory, and allowed for split-screen multitasking. We also added a keyboard component for upper grades and some options for keyboards at the lower grades. This honored the work of many teachers who have used the iPad to improve student learning in their classrooms for the past four or five years. It also reinforced the work we have been doing on the horizontal and vertical alignment of tools and curriculum within our district.

We sent this final communication out in a press release, a website, on social media, and via an all-community email. However, knowing that only a few people will read through an entire email, I decided to make an infographic outlining the process, the concerns, and the results (see Figure 4.2).

Using a combination of pictures and words to communicate can be powerful and appeals to many different types of end users. Although there are some programs online that can let you create these with little effort—Piktochart (piktochart.com) or Canva (canva.com), to name a few—I've found that creating my own using Keynote software on the Mac along with some creative commons icons from NounProject (nounproject.com) can be more flexible and unique.

Guidelines When Using Email

Email is still the primary preferred method of official communication among adults, even though we now seem to text more often than we email. If you are using email as your only form of communication, be sure to follow some basic guidelines when it comes to getting your message out there.

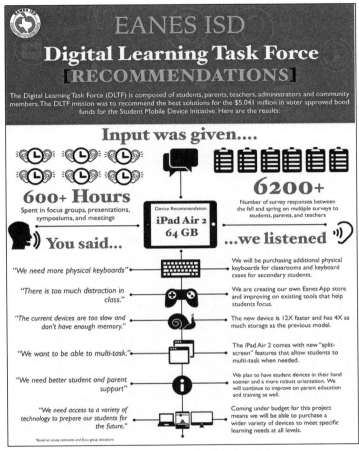

Figure 4.2 Infographic communicating final device choice.

No Scrolling

Receiving a lengthy email with a ton of text is already going to detract from much of the message when an end-user opens it. Try to keep the emails brief and without any scrolling necessary to get to the pertinent information. Consider taking out extraneous information to really make your point stand out.

Bullets!

Although too many bullet points in a presentation can be deadly, they can prove effective in an email communication. Get your point across in a series of bullets that:

- Communicate a timeline

- Communicate a reason

- Communicate any changes

Use Pictures

As I mentioned in the recommendation from the Digital Learning Task Force, using graphics, images, or infographics can quickly communicate a message in a way that catches the eye. Using a simple chart or photo of the end product or change can be quickly engaging and communicate a message.

Humor

As much as the internet meme has taken over parts of modern society, it does have a time and place. Using a meme or animated gif that ties to the message you are trying to communicate can add a bit of humor to what might otherwise be seen as an impersonal transaction between reader and sender. One tip: Put these at the end of your message so that email openers are required to at least scan your message with their eyes before being drawn down to the catchy meme or gif.

Don't Dilute the Inbox

I started this chapter by saying that communication can never be overdone. That said, sending multiple emails throughout a week can make people "deaf" to the sender in some ways. It's almost like a person who tells a lot of bad jokes. The first time it's kind of funny, but by about the fifth or sixth bad joke, you begin to avoid the person so as to not be subjected to any more bad humor. People who receive multiple emails from the same source often do the same thing—only it's easier to avoid an email than a person.

The Power of Video

Images and words can create an eye-catching message, but the power of video to relay a point or message can be captivating to the person on the receiving end. Although these take more time and production, the results can be a consistent message that is quickly digested (try to keep video messages to 2 to 3 minutes at most).

In the fall of 2012, we were rolling out our devices to the middle school classrooms and were trying to communicate the use and care of the iPads to our middle school students. Initially we put it on a piece of paper that came with the device. Then, we decided that we would also want to talk over the points on the paper with each class as we distributed the iPads. Our one major issue was that we didn't have enough staff to relay this message and to make sure that it was consistent.

Enter the power of video. We ended up creating a video (Figure 4.3) that would be played in each class to communicate our care and use of the device messages in a funny but informative way. Because the video was watched by every class, this created a common message and expectation around the use and handling of the device. Here's the video we displayed and the message it conveyed: mrhook.it/msipad.

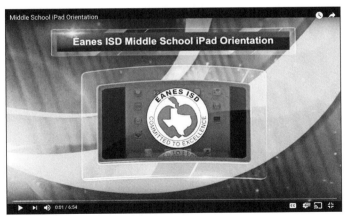

Figure 4.3 Eanes ISD Middle School iPad Orientation (mrhook.it/msipad).

Other Ways to Communicate

Mixing up the variety of ways you communicate can be effective as long as the messages overlap. Don't send out one message on Twitter, then a completely different one via email. Keeping the steady drip of the same message to your constituents means that they see your transparency and your consistency, which makes you a much more trustworthy source.

With the wide variety of electronic media out there, still one of the most tried and true methods of communication is face to face. As I mentioned earlier with the symposiums and focus groups, we gathered some invaluable information while we communicated our objectives and ideas. As a general rule of thumb, I try to get in front of a campus faculty meeting at least twice a year to talk about upcoming and current projects.

Spending 5 or 10 minutes in front of a group of staff makes you more approachable, but also keeps their attention and focus more than any form of electronic communication you can come up with. Even just making time to walk around campuses shows a level of transparency and a human element that many teachers don't see from technology departments. Suddenly, that voice on the other end of the line has a name and a face. The next time they receive a message from the technology department, they'll know who the person is and be more apt to hear what they have to say.

CHAPTER 5

KEYS TO A HAPPY MARRIAGE OF IT AND CURRICULUM

"The IT department always says 'No.'"

"The curriculum department is asking us to do the impossible with no resources."

Throughout the many districts I've visited during my years in education, these quotes seem to always crop up whenever a district is trying to expand its technology integration. The roles seem to quickly develop between the "evil" technology department and the "unrealistic" curriculum and instruction department. One of my former assistant superintendents once told me that conflict arises where there is a big difference in expectations between two parties.

The "marriage" between a technology services department and a curriculum and instruction department can be the thing that really makes a mobile device initiative successful—or makes it crash and burn. Each side has to overcome their own set of internal challenges as well as the expectations of the other side to make things work. In this chapter, I expand on this marriage analogy to really see the areas where growth and cohesiveness can come from.

Take Trips Together

One of the best ways to put a marriage to the test is to plan a trip together. My family likes to take a road trip every summer. We even create a hashtag for the trip (#hookertrek15 for example). Being in a van with three little kids over the course of two weeks can be extremely exhausting as well as rewarding. The purpose of the trip is to expand the experiences of our own kids as well as some family bonding.

That said, there are times when the road trips go awry. Like the time the carrier container on top of the van flew open without us knowing it, causing all our swimming gear to fly all over the I-35 freeway. Or the time we stopped at a vacant rest stop in Arkansas only to find out both why it was vacant and why they say the state bird of Arkansas is the mosquito. Maybe it's the Clark Griswold in me, but I sometimes enjoy the mishaps as much as the successes.

In the marriage of IT and C&I, the "big road trip" really happens when you decide to travel down the path of a mobile device initiative. Both parties have different expectations and destinations along the way. There will be times when your trip has a flat tire or when you are all just too cranky to talk to each other, but you have to persevere in order to reach the destination together.

During our road trip over the past six years, we have seen and done some amazing things together. We've also had our fair share of mishaps (see Chapter 2 on top 10 things not to do). Just as with a road trip, though, when we look back at how we reached our successes or when we were mired in failure, we can see that there was a correlation with planning and communication. Let me give you a recent example.

This past fall, we decided to purchase Apple TVs for each classroom. Knowing there was a fair amount of testing that needed to take place before we just installed one in every classroom, we discussed what would be the best course of action before we took this trip. The IT staff was stretched thin recovering from the start of school, and the curriculum and instruction staff were in midst of rolling out a new teacher evaluation system. Rather than just throw the devices out there with little support or time for training, we decided together to ask teachers to apply to be part of an Apple TV pilot program.

Being part of the pilot meant that you knew the technology was so new that it might not work right off the bat, and that you would be willing to provide feedback on areas where it might improve. In all, we had 150 teachers apply to be in the pilot, which was beyond our agreed capacity (we had targeted 50 as our goal), so we rolled the devices out in two phases to make sure we didn't stretch our bandwidth or stress our departments too much.

Part of planning a good road trip together is being able to identify different checkpoints and mini-goals along the way. You don't just get in the car and drive to the final destination (in our scenario, that final destination was an Apple TV in every classroom). Instead you build in various checkpoints to stop and take breaks and reassess before you continue forward. Communicating the goals between the departments for a rollout like mobile devices or digital curriculum implementation can make for much smoother road trips with fewer arguments and more happy moments versus stressful ones.

Have Kids

There is nothing more major in a relationship than the decision to have kids. This is not like buying a house, where you can move if you don't like it, or buying a car that you can sell if it's not quite your type. Having kids is a life decision that stays with you even after the marriage ends.

In the IT and C&I marriage, this really happens when you enter into the world of digital curriculum and resources. There is an expectation, and rightly so, that students and teachers will have immediate and continual access to resources purchased by the district. In the time before mobile devices, this meant that the curriculum and instruction department purchased textbooks and consumable workbooks while the IT department made sure the printers and projectors worked.

However, now that these resources are digital, there is a lot more pressure between the two departments to work together to make sure these tools work consistently. Much as with having kids, there are times when the "parents" need to talk about the best way to implement the tools and whether or not they are compatible with current or future systems.

Here's another example, this time a little more problematic, where we may have raised a problem child because we didn't communicate expectations correctly before purchasing a resource. About two years into our 1:1 iPad program, there was a major textbook adoption at the state level (this is a big thing in Texas, but I realize other states may not work this way). The state actually changed its approach by letting districts have "local control" over what they purchased as long as it helped teach the state standards.

A group of teachers gathered to look over the resources and landed on a particular science resource that they really liked. The only problem was, the digital component of the resource ran using Adobe Flash, which, as you may or may not know, doesn't play well with iPads. At no point during the adoption process (another child analogy) was the IT department involved for input. The curriculum and instruction department had just purchased an unsupported resource.

Districts just now entering into the mobile device world, whether it be 1:1 supported devices or bring your own device, need to make sure they are own the same page before adopting one of these "kids" that aren't supported. I will also say it works in both directions. When an IT department chooses a platform that is browser or device specific for certain programs, like a grade book or student information system (SIS), they make it more challenging for the curriculum and instruction department to find tools that fit on those specific platforms.

Going forward in the raising of these "kids" together, the best approach is one that includes constant and open communication as well as a level of device-agnostic digital resources. The hardware may change, so purchasing systems that can be used on multiple devices and browsers is ideal.

The other big issue besides hardware and software compatibility with digital resources is how the rosters and logins are created for students to access the tools. Unless you are going with completely open-source curriculum (which can be openly posted on the web), you'll likely have to manage some sort of codes or login files to make sure only certain classes have access to certain resources.

Depending on your SIS, there could be multiple ways to go about doing this. In some cases, the digital resource company will take a nightly upload of data to a specifically formatted .csv file. In other cases, students can use a third-party log-in like Google Apps for Education or Microsoft 365 to access the materials based on their email domain. There are now some third-party systems that help create a "handshake" between SIS and curricular resources (clever.com being probably the most prevalent in this field as of the writing of this book).

Regardless, when you decide to have these digital kids together, make sure you discuss how they are being accessed, who can access them, and what the expectations are for when they are being accessed. I will dive more deeply into how to actually see if they are being used for learning in Chapter 8, "R.O.L. = Return on Learning."

Get Advice from the In-Laws

When you marry someone, you also inherit their entire family in the form of in-laws. Some marriages are lucky enough to have supportive in-laws who help nurture and love the happy couple. Others are no so lucky, where you have in-laws who seek to destroy or ruin the relationship. Most marriages are somewhere in between, where in-laws will generally support and give advice when needed. Sometimes that advice can be unsolicited, but there are times when hearing another perspective can be valuable.

David Weinberger's quote, illustrated in Figure 5.1, is especially powerful when you think about the sharing of ideas and resources between IT departments and curriculum and instruction. Many of the people in these departments have connections within other districts or with districts where they may have worked previously.

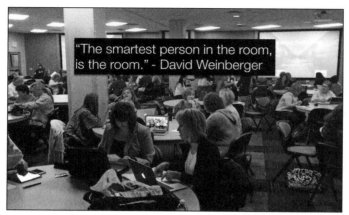

Figure 5.1 "The smartest person in the room, is the room."
—David Weinberger

One of my former colleagues, a technology services director, used to be teased whenever we would pose a problem and he would respond with, "Well, the way we did this in my previous district was this." Although we gave him a hard time for always referring to his former district, the knowledge and experience he brought with him from there was extremely useful. Why ignore the failures and successes of another district when embarking own your own journey? Much of the material I supply in this book series is my own perspective of failures and successes in the hopes that others may learn from them. These are not just my own, though. They come from visiting districts and leaders all over the country and hearing their stories and struggles.

When purchasing a digital resource, one of the first questions that a curriculum and instruction department or IT department might ask the vendor is,

"Where else have you implemented this resource? What other districts similar to ours are using it?" These questions as well as a list of reference districts can help better inform both parties in this marriage about the obstacles or challenges they might need to overcome to make it a success. As with in-laws, sometimes this advice comes unsolicited, but it doesn't hurt to listen if it helps bring the departments closer and ultimately helps students learn.

Spice Things Up

A marriage that is exactly the same, day in and day out, may sound like a stable relationship. However, it could also be seen as an uninspiring marriage. Couples often take trips, go on date nights, or try other methods to keep their marriage fresh and exciting.

Keeping that in mind and applying this analogy to the marriage of IT and C&I, there are times when doing the same thing the same way every time can actually cause problems down the road. Especially in the world of technology, there are ever-changing tools and resources that can optimize internal systems and make learning more visible for students and teachers.

Changing systems constantly is not advisable, but always keeping an eye on the future and planning for down the road can help propel a district forward. I've heard the saying that if someone went to sleep 120 years ago and woke up today, the only thing that would be the same is education. With the new revolution of mobile devices in the classrooms, I'd argue that that expression is quickly becoming false.

There will be times when you'll want to try something new or different that you think will help everyone in the district. When I first started in IT as a virtualization coordinator, my former boss was convinced that making all the desktops in the district virtual would extend the life of the devices, thus saving money and support. Although his theory made sense, the outcome left something to be desired.

Students could access the internet and other applications, but there was always a slight lag that caused end users to be frustrated with the experience.

Many just decided not to use the machines at all because of this frustration. Although this was a new idea, it wasn't really discussed with classroom teachers or the curriculum and instruction department (remember, communication is key). Although this may have spiced things up a bit for the IT department, it wasn't met with the greatest reaction from the curriculum and instruction side of the house, because it was never really discussed before it happened.

Deal with Arguments

As I remarked earlier, disagreements or arguments arise when there is a gap in expectations between two parties. There will be times when the IT department has to say "No" or "We can't support that." As someone who likes to please everyone, learning how to say no in a way that doesn't damage the relationship between the IT department and the curriculum and instruction department can take some work.

One of the most successful ways for me to overcome a situation where I have to tell a teacher or administrator no is to also come up with an alternative to their problem. For example, we had a situation arise in one of our middle schools where students were using the AirDrop feature to spread a rumor around with a fake image. The image was a fake arrest photo of a staff member at the school that had clearly been doctored with poor Photoshop skills.

When I arrived at the campus and heard the situation, the administration wanted us to immediately turn off the AirDrop functionality of all the iPads. Although this is something we could do, I wanted to also ask the administration what we were trying to accomplish by doing this. Immediately stopping the one way they were sharing the fake news would only have them continue this on a different platform or resource. The real goal of the administration was to educate kids on what was real and what wasn't when it came to news, social media, and the internet. We ended up turning off AirDrop temporarily, but also asked to talk with the students about this topic so it wouldn't continue to arise in other situations throughout their school career.

The easier thing to do in that situation would have been just to turn AirDrop off and walk away. In a marriage, sometimes you concede certain things just to make life easier. But there are also times when you have to dig your heels in and figure out what is best for both parties. There are also times when one side makes a mistake with a purchase or an implementation that causes grief or friction.

Much as I tell my own kids, owning the mistake and then coming up with a solution for the problem is much more effective than trying to cover it up and possibly lie about it. Open and honest communication creates a bond of trust between both parties that helps overcome petty arguments and actually helps with future goals and ideas when it comes to digital learning in your district.

CHAPTER 6

BUILDING AND SUPPORTING THE BACKBONE

R ecently I was driving down a two-lane road in the middle of central Texas. These rural roads are pretty prevalent in this state, as well as others, I imagine. On this day, I came up behind a "double-wide" mobile home being transported to a new location. My first inclination (after slowing down) was to figure out how to get around this behemoth of a vehicle. The shoulder was covered by the home, and the oncoming traffic was hard to see.

Rather than risk driving around the house on either side, I decided to patiently wait until the house turned or they pulled over. A few minutes later, I was rewarded as the vehicle pulled over to the shoulder to let the line of cars pass.

In some ways, the role of the technology department is much like that of the truck carrying the house. We sometimes need to hold back traffic on our networks in order to move large objects or prioritize what should and shouldn't pass. There are other times when we pull over and let others stream through the network without much holdup. Regardless of reasons, we also have to remember that whatever we are blocking or holding up affects a series of frustrated "drivers" of the network lining up in a queue behind us. This is why most technology departments try to plan any needed outages during the time with the least amount of traffic. Although the best-laid plans can often be disrupted, we do have to remember that every action has a reaction.

When we began our 1:1 in the summer of 2011, we knew that our infrastructure could not handle the load of all these new devices hitting our wireless access points. In fact, the spring before our initial rollout, we actually ran out of IP addresses to provide on our network at the high school, causing all sorts of problems. It turns out that even though we only "officially" had 600 devices at the high school, many of the 2,700 students were bringing their own and hitting our guest network, thus limiting the number of IP addresses we could lease out.

This incident couldn't have happened at a better time for us. We had funds in place for upgrades but weren't sure how powerfully or thoroughly we really needed to stretch our network to support the initiative. One thing was certain—the network needed to be optimized and also as fail-proof as possible *before* we handed out the first device.

Access

Although much of this book is based on mindset, there are some technical issues that need to be addressed in order to pull of a successful mobile device initiative. The company names may change, but one of the primary areas of support from a technology department is the wireless infrastructure.

A fairly large percentage (20%) of our initial mobile device initiative was dedicated to upgrading our wireless infrastructure and bandwidth. With more devices on the network and additional video resources such as YouTube SafeSearch, we knew our network traffic would hit a limit fairly quickly. Before the mobile device initiative, we had one access point for every four classrooms and a few extra in common areas. We knew that wouldn't be enough and that those APs would eventually choke in areas of high density.

We brought in network consultants to help us map out our wireless zones and figure out where the gaps and weaknesses would be. Common areas like the library and cafeteria actually needed even more access than before, as now students would be using these common spaces during their breaks or off-classes. We increased the number of access points to one per classroom, knowing that would be more than enough to cover the 30 to 40 devices in each room, but also with an eye toward the future.

With increased access points throughout the buildings, our choke points moved further down the infrastructure to our network closets and ultimately our backend controller, which was in serious need of updating. Bringing in equipment that could handle load-balancing and coupling that with software and a firewall that would allow us to traffic-shape and prioritize various items on the network, we were able to throttle up and down depending on the instructional need.

When rolling out a device initiative of any type, please do not overlook the wireless network load. I've seen many a device initiative go down in flames because a network couldn't handle the traffic. This is especially important when running cloud-based devices like Chromebooks that rely heavily on access to a network to be optimized.

Adaptability and Customizability

As I said in Chapter 1 of this book, we are not truly an "enterprise" when it comes to network and hardware solutions in education. Any system that is using technology to help with learning and teaching has a variety of tools that accomplish the necessary learning goals. Creating a system that is restrictive or limiting means that you are also creating a system that restricts and limits student learning.

Technology changes at such a rapid rate that any system not prepared to adapt will soon be considered archaic. When we rolled out our initial network filtering system, for example, all social media was being blocked by default. Even certain components of Google (which we use for collaboration) were blocked by the filter. Luckily, most filters today contain the ability to add exceptions or "white-list" certain sites.

We did, however, realize that making sweeping system-wide changes such as filters or the way to provision apps (which I'll get into more later in this chapter) can have a ripple effect on learning. Make sure that the right processes (addressed more in Chapter 7) are in place, along with open, consistent communication about the actual changes taking place (as discussed in Chapter 4).

Any holes in your system are quickly exposed when making a change such as adding a filtering policy or restricting certain types of applications. In our high school, we have an incubator course set up that runs very much like a start-up business. The teams of students work with actual business leaders and actual business tools, as this course is meant to be more of a real-world scenario than a simulation. One issue that quickly arose was that much of the start-up world used a tool called Slack (slack.com) to collaborate and share asynchronously.

Although email is still our supported system, we knew that the 150 or so students taking this course wanted to learn how to use exactly the same systems many start-up companies around them used. The easiest answer for us would have been to just say no and force them to continue to use our email as a way to communicate. However, because one of the goals of the course was to mirror the actual business world, we had to find another solution.

Our newest filtering software allowed for grouping of students into certain politics and restrictions. With Slack being a relatively new and untested system, we didn't want to open it up to the entire campus without some best practices being put forth and communicated. As a team, we had used Slack for almost a year as a way to reduce the hundreds of emails going back and forth that could be better managed using a channel on Slack. After communicating with the parents of these students in the incubator course, we were able to group those students into a certain policy group that allowed for the in-school testing of Slack. None of that is possible if you lock everything down into a standard system without flexibility.

Lock-Down Events

In the spring of 2013, we were finally finished with the distribution of our devices to all students. Every student, K–12, had a device in their hands. On April 15, 2013, the Boston Marathon bombing took place. This was just a few days after we had distributed the last device. Why was this significant? Now every student had access to watch the news (and in some cases carnage) unfold right in front of their eyes.

In a panic, one of the middle school principals contacted me and asked me to "turn off the internet" as students were seeing things like bloody body parts and people maimed from the explosion. While I like to think of myself as powerful, even I can't turn off the entire internet. I could however, shut down our wireless system to prevent the viewing of news articles and images from the event. In reality, considering that most students had mobile phones in their pockets that didn't need access to our network to get to the internet, this would have been a useless gesture.

Instead, we turned it into a teachable moment as the news unfolded in front of us. Teachers talked with students about their reactions and concerns as well as discussing what was real news and what was fake news (some reports had up to nine people with bombs running around Boston at the time).

There will almost certainly be a point during your mobile device initiative where a student attempts either to hack the system or to usurp the network in order to look at inappropriate content. Those issues can be handled with a mix of standard administrative discipline and individual restrictions of the device. However, on occasion there may be a global event like the Boston Marathon bombing that takes place during the school day. Unlike the events of 9/11, which unfolded mostly on the television in 2001, a major global event now cannot be hidden from our kids.

I will dive deeper into the ideas around policies and procedures in the next chapter, but as someone supporting the technology and network of a mobile device initiative, you'll want to meet with administration to come up with an action plan. Just as you would in the case of a bad weather situation, you want to have a plan for the students' devices in place in the event that a global situation arises.

The World of Mobile Device Management

One of the main reasons (besides financial resources) that a district promotes a student-owned or BYOD initiative rather than a school-issued device initiative is management of the devices. In our situation with iPads in 2011, there was little out there in the form of mobile device management (MDM) systems. We ended up using a system called JAMF (jamf.com) because it seemed to have the best features and was most supported by Apple.

In the Windows world, devices can be managed by logins that require someone to have a deeper knowledge of scripts and policy enforcement in the back end of the system. One of the reasons why Google's Chromebooks have really taken off in the world of mobile device initiatives is because of their cloud-based management console that easily allows you to group certain restrictions or push out various extensions to the end user.

Regardless of which device your district chooses for its mobile learning initiative, you will need a way to manage, track, and support it. Because the technology changes regularly, I won't spend much time going into which is the best for which device. However, I will make a few suggestions when it comes to the actual implementation of an MDM and who controls it.

When we started our 1:1, we had one person in control of the entire system from top to bottom. This meant that he alone had to be trained and up-to-date on the system, and that he was the only one who had access to it. The thinking there was that the fewer people who had access to a system, the less likely it was to fail.

The biggest issue with that mindset was that the person in charge of the MDM quickly becomes a choke point once you cross a certain threshold of devices. For us, our threshold was once we had more to support more than one campus with our 1:1 initiative. App requests and device tracking became more than a full-time job at certain times of the year.

During our second iteration of 1:1, we decided to change our way of thinking. Rather than having one person manage each and every part of the devices, we outsourced part of the management (in our case app provisioning) to the campus-level technicians and educational technologists. This did mean that there were now more cooks in the kitchen to potentially mess things up, but because our new system was so restrictive to start (we removed the App Store from the devices and hosted our own app store), we needed to have support from multiple points along the system.

The end result has been faster turnaround time on app requests and a much deeper understanding of the MDM system from staff throughout the district. Rather than having situations arise where "the MDM guy won't let me do that" or "the MDM guy is too busy," we now had end users on the campus level who could now see the process involved in provisioning apps and in turn took more ownership of the process.

Sustainability

Recently, my wife and I were shopping for new cars. We liked both of our current cars, but they were starting to get long in the tooth, and we had seen some newer, more high-tech features in cars hitting the market recently.

Buying a car is a major financial investment that depreciates over time. We have friends who like to lease their cars for this very reason. Rather than spending money owning a car that would be worth a lot less in three to four years, why not just pay a consistent monthly amount and then freely upgrade a few years down the road?

Both of these scenarios have their pros and cons. In one case, you actually own the car, so you can also sell it and recoup some of the expenses, albeit at a reduced value. In the other case, you can get a new car every few years, but you are locked into a continuous payment and really have nothing to show for it except a mode of transportation.

Buying technology and mobile devices very much mirrors this car-buying scenario. In one case, you can purchase technology and know that it depreciates almost instantly, but you will have something to show for it at the end. In the other case, you can lease the technology over time, which allows you to refresh devices at a much more rapid rate.

Supporting a mobile device initiative involves much more than even the focus areas of this six-book series. Administration and the community must be in agreement on the purpose and the "Why" of a program like this not only in order to get buy-in but also in order to allocate financial resources to make it successful and sustainable over time. This is another reason (besides management of the devices) that districts are so keen to have a student-owned or BYOD program.

Whether buying or leasing technology, you'll want to discuss with administration and the business office how to best maximize your financial resources to create a sustainable program. In Texas, depending on the social-economic demographics of your district, you could either be pulling in additional funds from the state or you could have funds "recaptured" to help fund those districts with lesser resources.

In our case, as we are in a district that gets a significant portion of funds recaptured, we knew we couldn't fund a 1:1 program with our maintenance and operations (M&O) budget alone. We elected to use a capital bond program instead and have the community vote to support the technology behind the program in a bond election. Of course, the danger of relying on that method is that a time may come when, for whatever reason, the community elects to not pass a bond. We also needed to make sure we had funds in place to help with repairs (covered more in the next section).

In districts with more funds provided by the state or their own M&O budget, a leasing model makes more sense. In that model, it's built into the budget just like electricity and internet. Of course, just like leasing a car, the downside is that you will be stuck paying monthly for devices that you will never truly own.

Some districts have figured out how to make a hybrid of a student-owned and school-issued device scenario with more of a "lease to own" option. As the laws vary in many states, I won't spend much time on this scenario, but I do see the value in having the students pay for a portion of the device over time and then, when they graduate, they can take it with them through a buy-back program.

Regardless of your financial situation, sustainability of technology is a major issue that needs to be addressed before you proceed too far down the road to a school-issued mobile device initiative.

To Insure, or Not to Insure … That Is the Question

Keeping the devices operational over time, especially when dealing with multiple users over multiple campuses, means having some repairs built into the budget. We tried many different scenarios to make this work for us when it came to family-purchased insurance. As we couldn't make the insurance mandatory for legal reasons, we wanted to make sure parents would see the value in having the insurance to help save on their own out-of-pocket repairs. When a student loses a textbook, they are required to pay back the entire cost of the book. In our case, as these devices are used for more than textbooks and more expensive, providing parents with options made the most sense (Figure 6.1).

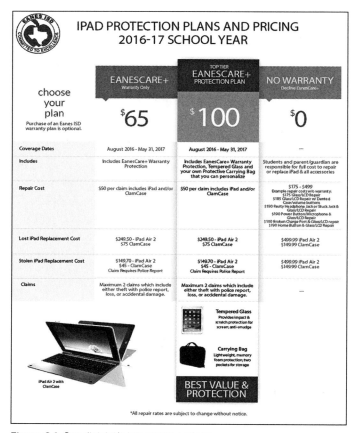

Figure 6.1 Our district's insurance options.

When it comes to insurance of the devices, you have two basic choices—to self-insure, or to pay a third-party company to insure the devices at a yearly cost. We tried both of these options in our first few years of implementation and discovered, somewhat painfully, that using a third-party company was not the best way to go. They required much more paperwork and had some strict timelines when it came to a device being lost or stolen, in which case we had to produce police reports before an initial date or the device would not be insured.

By self-insuring, we are able to build up a fund to pull repair money from or to purchase new devices in the case of a loss or theft. Different districts have different price points based on the device cost, the amount of time the students have the devices, and so on. For us, because students keep their devices year-round, we wanted to build in enough extra to support any that went missing over the summer as well as those dings, dents, and cracked screens that occurred during the school year.

Repairs and Asset Tracking

One final thing to mention in this chapter on support is to consider how you will be supporting the repairs of school-issued devices and how you'll track them as assets. In our situation, most of our iPad damage came when a screen was cracked (another reason why it's a good idea to spend a little bit extra on a protective case or offer extra protection to parents as I showed in Figure 6.1).

To help track the repairs and insurance, we document every incident in our student information system (SIS) under the student's name and then make a note if they carry the optional insurance coverage. Because these devices are being used heavily for instruction, we also have a small amount (around 3% to 5%) of "hot swaps" available for a student who has paid for a damaged or stolen device.

We originally had planned to use a group of student techs from the high school to help with the support and repairs of the devices. However, although we do have a group of student techs (or "minions" as they are affectionately called) who help with some of the technology issues, we found out through consulting with our legal department that we couldn't have them repair the screens. Many other districts have found success in having a small in-house repair shop that is run by the technology department but has student workers and extra parts to help facilitate any repairs or damages.

There are also now a growing number of third-party repair companies in the marketplace that make the process of repair simple and timely. Although there are many out there, the one we have found success with is iTurity (iturity.

com). Their setup is easy and they provide a postage-paid packaging box that we can send overnight to their shop and expect 48-hour turnaround on device repairs or swap-outs. As much as we want to try and minimize damage with a good case, it's always a good idea to have a company like iTurity in your back pocket, especially at times of high turnover (such as the end of the school year).

We also struggled early on with various asset tracking systems. Ultimately all of the students' assets (including textbooks) needed to be funneled into our student information system. Rather than pay for a third-party company to track the devices and repairs, then send the information to our SIS, we eliminated the middleman and created additional fields in the SIS to help with tracking. One downside of this to consider is that it does require a lot of front-end work from technicians (noting repairs), the business office (collecting insurance or repair payments), and in some cases the campus office staff that actually handles many of the transactions and entering of student data in the SIS.

Making a mobile device initiative successful takes much more than just the things covered in this chapter. However, without the proper wireless network, or a way to manage the devices, or a system for repairs and asset tracking, an initiative will fail before it ever gets started.

CHAPTER 7

POLICIES AND PROCEDURES

When I was growing up in the 1980s, there wasn't a lot of technology for my parents to deal with. With a Commodore 64 computer and some really entertaining games, my parents didn't spend a lot of time monitoring what I was doing or worrying about what mischief I might get into. We didn't have the internet, so there really wasn't any worry on that end. However, I learned quickly that there were "bootleg" copies of games I could get from friends.

As I wasn't really heavily monitored, that meant I could access a game that might have been borderline inappropriate and my parents would be none the wiser. The honest truth is that anything I did on that computer was minimal compared to the inappropriate stories and discussions shared among my teenage friends. Most of these stories involved some sort of body parts or flatulence that would have made my grandmother blush. The stories stayed within my circle of friends, as there was no social media to share them.

In 1985, my dad purchased a VHS recording over-the-shoulder video camera. This simple machine allowed me to capture my imagination in video form and either make up a fake news desk or recreate George Michael's "Faith" video. Have you ever thought, thank God YouTube didn't exist when I was a kid? (hand raised).

I grew up in a fairly strict household, with expectations for language, behavior, and attitude. However, there were never any rules, policies, or filters put in place when it came to technology use. Any punishment I ever received was because of my actions, not because of the technology. Recording my friends having a vulgar conversation with the video camera or playing a bootlegged game meant being grounded because of my intent.

I mention this here because in the modern era, technology is obviously much more ubiquitous but also treated as a means of punishment. Doing something inappropriate with your phone? Let me take that away. Searching something on YouTube you shouldn't be? Give me that laptop. Unlike when I was a child, the punishment is focused around the technology more than the intent or behavior.

Allowing devices in your schools or distributing them to students in a 1:1 means that you've now added a layer of complexity and access to those same questionable behaviors that I had as a kid, only now on a wider scale. There will be times during your mobile device initiative that you have to figure out what role technology plays as a punishment or reward for behavior. These are conversations that need to happen with campus administration, as they are generally the first responders to anything done inappropriately with technology in schools.

Discipline Problem or Technology Problem?

Going back to the story of my childhood, my actions are the things that got me into trouble. Students now have information and access at their fingertips, which means there will be more temptations to search or discover inappropriate content. I outlined one such scenario at the end of Chapter 5, with students spreading fake news via AirDrop, but here's another one.

Scenario

A student is using their school-issued device and school-issued email to tease another student, sending them silly messages, memes, and maybe even taking pictures of them without their permission in order to ridicule or "cyberbully" the other student. The first reaction of administration and even the parents would be to lock down their email or take their device away for a short period of time.

Although that might seem like the best course of action, it's wrong. Think about this question: Did taking away the technology or the tool address the problem? Or did it just stop the ease with which the problem could be spread?

I have run into many situations where the easiest decision is to take the device away or to turn off a student's email. Although those are certainly viable punishments in extreme cases, they don't address the real problem: that one student feels that it is appropriate for them to verbally and emotionally abuse another student. The intent was never dealt with, only the method of delivery. It's like solving someone's addiction to smoking by just taking away the cigarette they are smoking at the time. You never actually discussed the ills of smoking; you just took away one of the methods by which they are getting the nicotine into their system.

One thing that is greatly helped with transparent and continuous communication is the role of the technology department when it comes to student discipline issues. Cyberbullying is just bullying made easier by the anonymity and access of technology. Looking at inappropriate images is something that has taken place for generations, but instead of magazines now it's much faster by just typing in a quick search term. Technology has not caused inappropriate behavior, but it has certainly amplified it. In some ways, technology actually helps identify these actions and behaviors as it captures a record of what has occurred.

Except for extreme cases, any behavioral issues that arise or are discovered as a result of your student mobile device initiative must be dealt with while keeping the intent in mind. A discipline issue with technology should be handled the same way on a campus as a discipline issue that happens without technology.

AUP or RUG?

Technology can both cause and solve a great many problems. When I started in my current position, we had an acceptable use policy (AUP) that addressed the use of hardwired desktop computers on our network, but little else. It was so specific that when smartphones began showing up on our campuses, we had no real way to police or support the use of student-owned devices in the classroom.

One of the other problems with the AUP was that it was a set of "gotchas" that really only came into play after the action had taken place. Students only got in trouble after they did something they weren't supposed to and then happened to get caught. We wanted something that was proactive rather than reactive. We wanted something that put more of the ownership of actions on the student rather than the administrator or technology department catching a student in the act.

We decided to change the nomenclature of the document from acceptable use policy to responsible use guidelines (RUG). Even this subtle title change placed an emphasis on the role of the student and their "responsibility" when handling any technology throughout the district. An example is the preamble of sorts from our current RUG (you can find the complete high school version of our RUG here: mrhook.it/whsrug)

Our staff and students use technology to learn. Technology is essential to facilitate the creative problem solving, information fluency, communication and collaboration that we see in today's global economy. While we want our students to be active contributors in our connected world, we also want them to be safe, legal, and responsible. The Responsible Use Guidelines (RUG) support our vision of responsible technology use and promote a strong sense of digital citizenship. The RUG applies to all Eanes Independent School District computer networks (including the devices made available by them), and all devices connected to those networks (whether they be student owned or otherwise).

With the ability to use technology comes responsibility. It is important that you read and discuss the District Responsible Use Guidelines, ask questions if you need help in understanding them, and sign the agreement form. It will be your responsibility to follow the rules for appropriate use. Irresponsible system use will result in the loss of the privilege of using this educational and administrative tool. Please review the leveled-guidelines following this document which breaks down in greater detail responsible use expectations for elementary, middle school, and high school students in the areas of Internet Safety & Security, Digital Citizenship, and Research & Information Literacy.

Please note that the Internet is a network of many types of communication and information networks. It is possible that you may run across some material you might find objectionable. While Eanes ISD will use filtering technology to restrict access to such material, it is not possible to absolutely prevent such access. It will be your responsibility to follow the rules for appropriate use. We require that students use the district-issued tablet as a baseline for instruction in the classroom. However, students are also allowed to bring a supplemental device in addition to the school-issued tablet. Please know that student-owned devices are not eligible for technical support and must adhere to these Responsible Use Guidelines while on school grounds. These responsibilities can extend beyond the school grounds when working on district platforms and systems from home. The school is not responsible for students who bring their own internet connectivity via air-cards or data-plan on a mobile device.

While the subsequent part of the RUG goes on to outline specific actions of both responsible and irresponsible use, I want to highlight a couple of changes we made because we were now a district that supports and encourages mobile learning. We know that students access our digital resources 24/7, so having an RUG that only addresses things like "when in school" can place some limitations on the student's expected responsibilities. As a result, we made sure to include verbiage that stated, "These responsibilities can extend beyond the school grounds when working on district platforms and systems from home." This shows that we expect this responsible behavior even when they leave our building.

In the real world, we know that people carry multiple devices on them to perform a variety of tasks. One area that we struggled with was the difference between the devices supported by the district and those student-owned devices like smartphones and laptops that made their way onto our campus. Students quickly discovered with the previous AUP that they could use their phone as a hot-spot to get around whatever filters in place and still not get in trouble for looking up inappropriate content because our AUP only covered district devices and network. To help get across the message that we expected responsible behavior regardless of device, we added in this section: *"Please know that student-owned devices are not eligible for technical support and must adhere to these responsible use guidelines while on school grounds."* Students can still bring in their own devices, but now they know that whether they use their own cell signal or our network, their actions have consequences.

Loan Agreement versus Best Practices

Over the course of our previous mobile device initiative, we saw that some students opted not to use the school-issued device because they felt too limited by the restrictions we had put in place. This provided a unique challenge because the classroom teacher expected every student to come in with a similar fully charged device. When students began opting out or bringing their own, teachers started to become frustrated because there would be days where not all students would have a device other than their phones with them. Schools in BYOD environments are very use to this experience and can adjust, but when the expectation in a 1:1 environment is that every student comes with the same device, it can cause problems when it comes to classroom instruction.

We originally had students and parents sign a loan agreement that outlined what could and couldn't happen with the device, but as we saw the need for more consistency in the classroom experience, we changed this document to best practices with the school-issued device. You'll also notice from the section of the RUG that we now require students to take the school-issued device as an instructional tool (much like a textbook, band instrument, or pencil) so that we can fully support the learning taking place on the device and reduce variation.

This best practices document (shared here: http://mrhook.it/best) gave us another opportunity to reinforce the roles and responsibilities of the student as well as the parents in this effort. Our preamble also reinforced the purpose behind using the device in the classroom:

> Eanes ISD uses Instructional Technology as one way of enhancing the mission to prepare and inspire all students for life-long success by teaching the skills, knowledge and behaviors students will need as responsible citizens in the global community. Students learn collaboration, communication, creativity and critical thinking in a variety of ways throughout the school day. Excellence in education requires that technology is seamlessly integrated throughout the education program. In an effort to increase access to those 21st century skills, EISD has made it a goal to offer students 24/7 accessibility to their learning. The individual use of technology is a way to empower students to maximize their full potential and to prepare them for college and the workplace.

> An important component will be education about digital citizenship and appropriate online behaviors. We will review cyber-safety rules with students frequently throughout the school year, and will offer reminders and reinforcement about safe online behaviors.

All students and parents/guardians must adhere to the Student Code of Conduct, Student Handbook, Responsible Use Guidelines, Board policies, and federal/state laws. In addition to those policies, we also recommend you review this document with your child.

The remaining sections go on to outline the student responsibilities when handling the device, including the expectation that it show up at school fully charged every day. We also wanted to make sure that students were backing up their data in our cloud storage system (Google Drive) in case something happened to their device.

In addition to these expectations, we outlined some parent responsibilities as well. As we do not filter the devices completely at home, we wanted to make sure parents were aware that they must help with monitoring device use at home and also to help remind them to charge their device nightly.

Device Contracts

Another idea to support the behaviors and policies of usage of a school-issued device or even student-owned device is to have a device contract of some sort for the students to sign. Using the word "contract" versus "best practices" can provide a little more firm language and add a layer of agreement between the student and the school.

In the book series focused on campus administration, I went into greater detail about how to work with the technology department on creating an agreeable and supportable expectation for students. Working with leadership on a behavior plan with technology and clearly stating that with students will go a long way toward avoiding some of the classic pitfalls of inappropriate usage. Having students sign a form or oath of some sort that states they will use the technology appropriately also places greater responsibility on their shoulders.

Our middle schools really valued this extra documentation on top of our best practices and RUG. This specific iPad Oath (Figure 7.1) outlined not only the expected behavior but also the consequences of breaking those expectations (Figure 7.2).

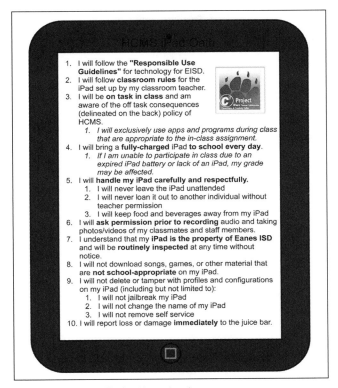

Figure 7.1 Sample iPad oath contract.

These graphics and the original idea for these oath agreements came from one of our amazing educational technologists, Lisa Johnson (@techchef4u), whom I've mentioned many times in this series. For a background on how she created these oath agreements, read here: mrhook.it/ipadoath. Lisa does a great job of graphically organizing the rules and lays out the expectations (and consequences) for students in a way that communicates them simply and effectively on a single sheet (front and back) of paper. The actual PDF version of the oath can be found here: mrhook.it/oath.

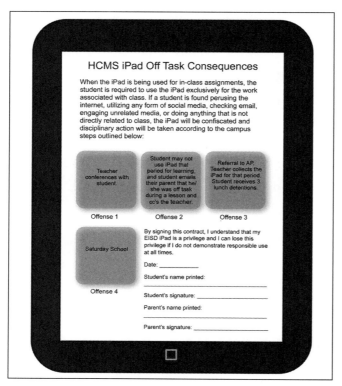

Figure 7.2 Consequences of iPad oath agreement.

The Extreme Scenario

No matter how clearly you outline the policies and expectations, that doesn't mean you will have all students and staff using technology responsibility. Many of the leaders and teachers in our district meet to discuss filters and technology behaviors so that we can somewhat proactively take action against certain issues. Although this constant flow of communication and collaboration with internal staff as well as parents does help prevent any major issues, there will be times when a student goes to the extreme and does something completely inappropriate with their school-issued device.

I describe in book 5 (the parent book) of the series how during one of our parent nights, a dad mentioned to me that his 16-year old son was taking the device up to his bedroom at night and closing the door. When I asked him if he had
a home filter, he said he didn't and asked if he should be worried about what his son might be doing. A 16-year old boy with unfiltered access to the internet should set off some red flags. In this case, I knew that certain parents had the expectation that the devices would be continually filtered and monitored even though we stated in all our paperwork and policies that this wasn't the case.

In one very extreme case, we had a student in one of our middle schools who was addicted to gaming—so much so that he even realized he had a problem and would come into class and place his iPad on the teacher's desk because he "couldn't handle the temptation." The parents and teachers were extremely frustrated because they knew there was some value in using the tool for learning, but the negative behaviors affected its use.

Your RUG or device agreement will take care of 99% of all issues when it comes to the use of your devices or student-owned devices. However, there will be cases like the ones above that arise in your school district. There is no blanket "correct response" for either of these scenarios or others that you might encounter.

What I've discovered over the years of doing this is the best resolution usually comes from getting all interested parties in the same room to discuss how to best solve the problem. In the cases just described, I immediately looped in the campus administration and in some cases the counselor, too, to get together with the parents and see if there was an accommodation or action plan that could be made to help the student.

Creating sound policies and documents and keeping constant communication between all stakeholders will help you proactively avoid any major issues during your mobile device initiative. But sometimes in extreme cases, the best plan is you just sitting down together to figure out the best plan of action that helps with the student's learning goals.

CHAPTER 8

R.O.L. = RETURN ON LEARNING

When I taught first grade (see Figure 8.1) at the turn of the century (which sounds like a lifetime ago), I had the benefit of having four Compaq desktop computers in my room, did all the other first grade teachers on my team. These machines were beasts. They took several minutes to start up, so often I would come in first thing and power them up so that by the times the kids arrived a half-hour later they would be ready to use.

I used them for a variety of purposes. One computer would be set up to freely create anything the student chose using a program called ClarisWorks. The others usually contained some sort of CD-ROM driven game like Reader Rabbit or Oregon Trail. (It's a fact that when you ask people about Oregon Trail and the number of ways to die, that "amoebic dysentery" is the number one answer.)

2001   CASEY ELEMENTARY SCHOOL   2002
MR. HOOKER - GRADE 1

Figure 8.1 My first experience teaching 21st-century learners.

At any rate, I had these computers set up as centers with the hopes that they would both engage the students and teach them a thing or two. Over time, I could tell some things were sticking, like the phrase "You died of amoebic dysentery," so I figured they must be learning something. Indeed, many of the "drill and kill" programs for math facts seemed to stick pretty well in students' memories whenever the time came to assess them.

But did I truly know those programs had an effect on learning? And if they did, why weren't others on my first grade team using them? Over the course of my time teaching, I discovered that the best program for learning and inspiring creativity was ClarisWorks. It didn't have any fancy animations or graphics, but it provided a blank canvas with a variety of tools for students to use to help them create something. Eventually, it became the go-to program on all four of my beastly machines, and students would earn points for an opportunity to create something to demonstrate their learning.

Flash forward to a decade or so later. We are rolling out iPads to the elementary schools, and many teachers are asking for a slew of consumptive "drill and kill" gaming apps to help students with practice and development. Much like my experience in the early 2000s, students were instantly engaged in these games, but that engagement waned over time. Students wanted more interactive and creative ways to demonstrate their learning.

Although I think there is a balance between consumptive and creative apps, the one thing that always troubled me, even back in 2000, was the fact that we never really knew how these programs were being used and that the others on my team weren't necessarily using them at all. There was no consistency and no data on whether there was a true "return on learning" (R.O.L.) because of the use of these programs.

Vetting Digital Resources

As I mentioned in Chapter 2, we decided in the fall of 2016 to shut down the App Store on our devices. This meant that we were now the conduit of all apps to the devices. We discovered quickly that with this fine layer of oversight many of our schools were requesting similar apps that did similar things but weren't aware of it. When we shut down the previous system, we found that more than 600 different applications had been requested by teachers over the course of a couple of years.

With this new system in place, we needed an "app vetting process" of sorts to make sure that our students were getting high-quality educational apps and that we weren't supporting too many similar resources. This process entailed teachers and students filling out a request form (here's an example: mrhook.it/appstore), which then triggered an alert to a team of instructional coaches and educational technologists to check the resource and decide if it was a high-quality application.

This process brought to light the quantity of resources we were using that really had no educational vetting. It made us tighten up our process to make sure that apps that were put on our devices aligned with our educational vision. The next challenge came in the form of curriculum resources. Many of our textbook adoptions come with some form of digital resource. However, when these are being evaluated, it's from the lens of the content that is in the resource, not with an eye to whether the digital aspect of the resource is even compatible with our systems and hardware.

When Curriculum and Technology Don't Talk

Creating the vetting process like the one mentioned above was great, but it started with the technology (in our case devices) in mind first and then checked whether or not the app was educationally appropriate. Imagine what happens when the roles are reversed. What happens when a curricular resource is purchased with no vetting on whether or not the technology is appropriate?

When we started our 1:1 iPad program, some of the curricula that were purchased contained digital content that ran with Flash (not supported on iOS devices) or were accompanied by some sort of onboarding process that the companies themselves hadn't quite figured out because they were publishers, not programmers.

As you might imagine, use of the resources that were non-compatible became impossible. During the vetting of the materials, no one from the technology side of the house was present to check on those compatibility features, and because the technology was so new, those vetting the curriculum were not even aware it was an issue.

In some cases, the curricular resources may have been compatible with our devices, but weren't able to be delivered to students because they required some additional steps to put rosters into the system for students to gain access. This additional step, although seemingly small, can cause tremendous challenges for both teacher and technology department. Teachers want the digital resources right away, but sometimes because of school and course scheduling, the rosters aren't set until a few days before school starts.

Add to the mix that the companies selling the resources (the textbook companies) usually do not include an onboarding processes in the purchase. They issue you a list of redeemable codes or a set of generic logins and passwords, but they don't sync with any of your existing student management or learning management systems. That means extra hours of support or outsourcing programmers for help.

Whatever the reason, it's imperative that technology departments be involved in the early part of the curriculum adoption process to try to avoid these pitfalls before they happen.

Use of Digital Resources

One of the first actions I took in my new role of Director of Instructional Technology in 2010 was to look over the digital resources we were paying for and how they were being used. One such system (which will remain nameless) was a video tutorial program that showed short videos of how to use a variety of software. Although I liked the system and the interface, when I looked at the data, I saw that 27 of my 650 staff members had actually logged in and used it the previous year. This was an $11,000 system that was being used by a handful of staff, and even of those staff, maybe fewer than 10 were using it regularly.

I used this data to drive the decision to cut the program from a site license to a handful of individual licenses for those remaining super-users and save us over $9,000 in the process. I did this without any input from others (breaking one of my rules about communication in the process) and sat back waiting for the fallout from people no longer able to access the tool. A crazy thing happened.

Nothing.

No one cried out or complained that they weren't able to use the service, because in essence they never used it. I continued to do this for other systems in an attempt to "sunset" those that we weren't using regularly or effectively. Although I did encounter some headaches, I discovered a major flaw in how districts deal with educational technology. Most of these programs were set up on yearly renewals with little to no oversight of their use. It's like taking all those CD-ROM games from my first grade classroom, paying for them, and then putting them in the closet for the rest of the year.

I have spent the past several years trying to figure out ways to vet the use of the digital resources we have purchased. For the sake of this chapter, when I mention "digital resource," I'm defining it as any type of application or website that is accessed by students and teachers. These can be apps on devices or curriculum materials that just happen to be in digital form.

Just Because You Paid for It Doesn't Mean It's Good

As I mentioned earlier in this chapter, simply paying for a digital resource doesn't mean it actually works at improving learning. There is often a (false) assumption that you have to pay a lot of money for a high-quality instructional resource. Textbook companies have cornered the market on this ideology by providing access to information and charging districts hundreds of thousands of dollars to access it.

While these companies continue to get paid, there are actually an increasing number of Open Educational Resources (OER) available to schools that provide information digitally at no cost. Websites like OER Commons (oercommons.org) and CK12 (ck-12.org) have hundreds of curricular resources and textbooks available that align with many state and national standards.

And the added bonus of OER is that because they are open and free, they can be accessed by anyone, anywhere. So the days of uploading roster files or syncing a digital subscription with your active directory could be gone if gaining access to these resources only involves placing a link on a public website. Although the lack of cost and ease of support of OER should drive many districts toward utilizing it, many still have fear that because you don't pay for it, it must not be good.

Just Because It's Free or Inexpensive Doesn't Mean It's Good

This introduces the counterargument to the section above. Free or inexpensive doesn't always mean good. Many schools are faced with financial challenges that drive them to make decisions based on money and not what is educationally appropriate.

I worked with a district a few years ago that was faced with this very challenge when they were looking to increase the number of laptops for labs in their schools. There were two models they were considering. Each had its pros and cons, as often happens when you start debating types of devices. One was a relatively inexpensive "netbook" (a smaller laptop that was about $300 less than the other model), but it was fairly new and hadn't really been tested in an educational setting. The other was more expensive but had a long track record of success in education and tended to have a longer useful life than the less expensive model.

So what did the district decide? They chose the less expensive model so they could buy more devices, even though they knew that model was inferior to the other. Rather than choosing what we knew would be the more successful and longer-lasting device, they let money and price determine their choice. The thousands of netbooks they purchased proved to be problematic to support and also seemed to be unused in an educational setting. In an effort to save money, the district actually wasted it because these devices ended up stored in carts in closets all over the district. After three years they were deemed obsolete and removed from the district inventory.

Sometimes, making the best deal isn't going with the cheapest option—it's going along with the most efficient and effective use of your funds to support learning.

How Do You Know If a Resource Is Successful?

So let's say you have vetted resources and purchased the appropriate technology to support learning. How do you know if it's actually being used successfully? As in my first grade classroom, although I saw some anecdotal firsthand success with the programs we were using, I didn't have a lot of data to back it up.

Success of a program or initiative needs to be defined before the first purchase is ever made. Identify with a team what will define that success first, then be sure to evaluate it over the course of time. Some of that evaluation can come with usage statistics, whereas other data points could be learning outcomes or assessment data.

Where and How Do You Gather Data?

Identifying what data you will use to make your educational decisions is only the first step. Once a system is in place, you need to continue researching and assessing its use. The $11,000 program I mentioned earlier in the chapter had been used for years by just a handful of staff and renewed every year without data to back up the purchase. When staff were asked about the use of a program, the response might be, "Yeah, we think people are using it" or "Oh yeah, I know a teacher who uses it a lot." Both of these are perceptions of use without actual data to back them up.

As I started to investigate the usage statistics of our digital resources, I was faced with a major challenge: trying to interface with more than 30 systems, each with a set of unique administrator logins and a variety of reports. After several days of finding the administrator credentials, I discovered that some systems tracked use in real time while others required a couple of days to generate a report via an Excel file that would be emailed to me.

Even then, after I gathered all the usage data from all the systems, I didn't have anything to compare it to. No data from the past, no comparative data from similar systems. In my interview in Chapter 3 with CIO Leo Brehm, he mentioned how education is really bad with data. Everything lives in silos and none of the data really talks to each other. You have a learning management system (LMS) that barely talks to your student information system (SIS). On top of that, you have loads of digital tools and resources that don't talk to anybody. It's really hard to paint an accurate portrayal of the learner and their progress when this information sits in a variety of places that don't communicate or provide the whole picture.

I was wrestling with this dilemma in the spring of 2016 when I was approached by a company that was working on making all of this data available in an easy-to-read format. It seemed too good to be true, but instantly I was intrigued.

The company, called CatchOn (getcatchon.com), took all the data from multiple sources and compiled it into an easy-to-read dashboard (Figure 8.2). I fell so much in love with the system that I offered up my free time to help advise and even shape the product in return for using it to help my own district make decisions on products. I finally had access to the usage data of a multitude of digital resources at my fingertips (it even appeared on my phone!) and I could make more informed decisions going forward about renewals and purchases.

Figure 8.2 An early look at the CatchOn "App Insight" dashboard.

Once You Have the Data, What Do You Do with It?

The next big question to answer here is once you actually get the data easily enough, what do you do with that information? The first thing I did was identify programs that we weren't using very heavily but might have been paying heavily for. Once I separated out those programs with a very low return on investment (ROI) in terms of use, there were essentially two choices: either keep it or dump it.

Programs that showed a trend of low use and weren't really required by the state or district would need to be scrutinized more closely before completely dumping the program. Was the program not being used because there was lack of training or support? Or maybe staff weren't even aware of the resource. It's easy to fall into the trap of supporting multiple programs that do the same thing. Most teachers will not use multiple types of the same program, nor should you expect them to. However, most teachers will use an effective program if it hits on the following points:

- It's easy to use and navigate

- It's easy for the students to use and navigate

- Login is simple or through a single-sign-on (SSO)

- The backend data is easily accessible and useful for the teacher.

Having just a handful of programs that hit these bullet points can really hit a create opportunities for student learning and formative assessment.

So in scrutinizing those programs, it's possible that some weren't being used because they weren't very useful or they didn't hit on any of the bullet points above. These were fairly easy to cut out of the system, letting us find alternatives that were user-friendly and learner-centered.

Others were being used, but not very heavily because of lack of awareness or training. For these we made sure to increase awareness through our campus educational technologists and instructional coaches. Once there was awareness of a program, we went into the classroom to showcase its educational value to the teacher and students. This, in turn, increased the ROI of the program and improved the learning goals for the students.

In a few situations, such as with digital textbooks, dumping a program is not really an option. Digital textbooks from the major publishers usually require a substantial amount of up-front costs be paid even in advance of use. Once in place, the onus of making sure the programs were being accessed was on the district and teachers. Unfortunately, in some cases, these programs were not very user friendly (they didn't hit on any of the bullet points from above), so teachers and students would abandon them after early frustrations.

In the case of these mandatory, or pre-paid, resources, the best thing a district can do is work with the company and the teachers to make it work in the curriculum in a way that supports the learning. Then, in the future, prior to purchase, they should really analyze the way in which the program is being accessed, and make future financial decisions based not only on if a program has great content, but on whether it is also easy to onboard and access.

Finding Trends and Staying Ahead of the Curve

The one given in technology is that there is always something new right around the corner. When the world of online quiz games took off with Kahoot! (getkahoot.com) in 2014, almost immediately there were a few other companies whose programs did similar things with different features. In the online application and digital resource world, this is a constantly changing landscape.

On the one hand, you want to be aware of the systems you currently have and what objectives they are covering for student learning. On the other hand, you also have to keep an eye on the future and see what kinds of programs out there might help further student learning, engagement, and retention.

The other useful part of a program like CatchOn is that it can show you what other systems and programs your users are accessing. As a district leader in educational technology, one of the best ways to onboard a program is to have the teachers and students already using it. In the case of choosing Google Classroom as our LMS of choice, the data showed us that a large number (nearly 20%) of our secondary staff were already using it as an LMS even though we had paid for and were supporting a completely different platform. Furthermore, the data also showed that number was gradually increasing every month.

Having that kind of data and information can be invaluable. The end users were obviously voting with their logins as to which platform they felt hit on those user-interface (UI) and user-experience (UX) bullet points. Google Classroom accomplished the majority of what they wanted, so rather than forcing them to go back to the district's paid-for service that didn't have the UI or UX they desired, we made the transition to supporting Google Classroom across the district the following year. What made this even more powerful was that we had 80 to 100 teachers already using it, so we could tap them on the shoulder and ask them to showcase how they are using the program with members of their professional learning community (PLC) or grade-level team.

The truth is, we'll never be able to truly stay ahead of the trends when it comes to educational technology resources. However, if we can access the data easily enough, we can see more global and regional trends so we can adjust accordingly. "Listening" to the data and responding to it will have a more powerful impact for your students than ignoring it and staying with the status quo year in and year out.

CHAPTER 9

TYING IT ALL TOGETHER

I n the previous five books in this series, I've always used the space in this chapter to outline the ways in which each of the groups can work with each other. During the interview with Leo Brehm in Chapter 3, he mentioned how he wished a "Point of View" gun like the one from *The Hitchhiker's Guide to the Galaxy* existed. You could blast someone with the gun and they would instantly see the other person's perspective on things. The point of this chapter in all the books is so that each stakeholder can see the others' perspective when it comes to a mobile learning initiative. From district administrator to parent to teacher to coach, not having that perspective and communication can really hinder the progress of an initiative going forward.

District Administration

The goal of the district administration is to build and support the vision to all parties. Sometimes that may mean making a universal decision that affects the network or the way the technology department supports a project. In a perfect situation, the technology department is represented on a cabinet level or at least brought in whenever plans or ideas are raised that can impact how technology is supported in the district.

Although this doesn't have to happen on a regular basis, there should be a point at least once a semester where, as a technology department, you make or give a status report to the superintendent and possibly the school board. These may seem laborious at times, but they keep all parties on the same page, and when the time comes to ask for more financial support for a project, the people who make those decisions are already in the loop.

In general, as someone who worked on the technology side of the house for a couple of years, I would say that having the support of the superintendent and other district leaders can really make or break an initiative before it even gets off the ground. If they don't understand the "why" in what you are trying to do, they will not be able to stand in front of a group of community members or campus staff and state why you're doing what you are doing.

The example I used in Chapter 2 about the "Death of GroupWise" and how that was nearly upended because the superintendent didn't like the new format of Gmail was a perfect example of the importance of explaining the change to district administration. The superintendent did not like the interface of the new system, but she did understand the need to switch to a cloud-based email system. Had she not had the understanding of the "why," the entire system could have been squashed before it ever got off the ground.

Campus Administration

I've hit on this point in multiple chapters in this book as well as the book for administrators, but sitting down and communicating which issues are technical (like fixing devices or the wireless) versus which issues are behavioral (like bullying) needs to be a constant and ongoing communication.

The campus administrator is on the front line and often the first to hear about technical or behavioral issues. In a technology department, there needs to be an agreed-upon expectation about how each issue is dealt with in general. Although there are always exceptions that may require additional intervention, your main job is to support the successful use of technology and mobile devices on a campus.

Part of this happens even before the mobile devices arrive on a campus. Planning a schoolwide distribution of devices is the true first test in the relationship between IT and campus administration. When and where the devices be distributed? Which teachers will be affected by this? How will the parents and students get the necessary forms? Who will collect optional insurance? What if a student refuses the device in the case of a school-issued 1:1?

These questions should be addressed a few weeks before the day the devices are distributed. When that day finally does arrive, it takes an all-hands-on-deck approach. When we rolled devices out at our elementary schools, because the students were not taking the devices home, it involved an extra layer of planning with the maintenance department as we decided to build and install our own storage racks (Figure 9.1). The campus administration helped coordinate that discussion with maintenance and also with the classroom teachers so they understood why a particularly large piece of furniture was now being added to each room. Without their support, with parents and teachers in particular, the IT department will continue to be the "evil bad guy" rather than the "support" department.

Figure 9.1 Our custom-built iPad storage shelves.

Teachers

"I can't teach today—my projector is dead."

I mentioned this quote in the introductory section of this book. As crazy as that statement sounds, the reality is that working technology has now become a classroom expectation. Years ago, when technology was brand-new, most teachers were still trying to figure out how it fit in their traditional curriculum and instruction. As Leo Brehm mentioned in his Chapter 3 interview, technology was thought of as the "garnish" on the side of the main course of learning.

Now, with the expectation that technology always works, like electricity and air conditioning (especially here in Texas), the relationship between IT and the classroom teacher has to be seen as one of support and understanding. There needs to be a system in place for teachers to easily contact technology support and report problems or issues. Similarly, there needs to be an easy way for technology support to acknowledge the issues to the teacher and create a timeline of expectations for repair. System-wide changes may seem minor to a technology department but can be a major pain for the end user. Installing those iPad charging stations (see Figure 9.1) may not seem like a big deal, but they do require a teacher to find room in their classroom for something that may take up quite a lot of space.

When it comes to repairs and work order requests, we try to turn around all of ours within 48 hours. Obviously there are always exceptions, but as a general rule of thumb, we close out about 75% of our work orders in less than that amount of time. Part of this process is communicating with the teacher about the issue, and the other is prioritizing which issues are of the most pressing need. That can sometimes be difficult based on the personality of the end user.

For example, you could have one teacher who is pretty laid back and asking that you fix their projector so they can showcase some student work on the big screen. You might have another teacher who tends to stress out quite a bit and is extremely eager to print a report for themselves (even though they can view it digitally), but their printer isn't working.

In both of these cases, there is a need for repair. However, if you look at what they both want to accomplish and what potential work-arounds exist, the teacher with the projector outage is trying to do something that showcases student learning and only really has a single way (the projector) to do this. In the case of the print-happy teacher, the report exists only for him or her and can still be viewed digitally or printed on another printer down the hall.

Deciding how to prioritize these shouldn't be left to the person who manages the technicians or repairs. There should be input from the campus, from a principal, librarian, or educational technologist. When we started letting those instructional staff have input into prioritization of repairs, we saw that teachers were much more satisfied and felt much more supported by the technology department in general.

Professional Learning

Interfaces and programs change constantly in the technology world. Part of making the changeover to a new program or interface successful is working with instructional coaches on how to train staff on the new changes. Simply sending out an email with a list of what to do doesn't really cut it today. Having a good partnership with district trainers means that messages are communicated more effectively, thus helping reduce frustrations and work orders based on a lack of understanding.

One thing that Apple likes to do is to release major iOS updates in September right after the school year starts and teachers and students are already comfortable with the existing operating system. As a district, we know we need to eventually move everyone onto the new OS, but ask that teachers and students refrain from updating until the kinks and bugs are worked out (that usually comes with the ".1" release of said operating system).

During that timeframe, the technology department is working with the educational technology department to test out functionality of existing apps and resources. The educational technology department is testing out the new features of the operating system and determining which, if any, can help in the classroom. Throughout this "window" of updating, there is a constant back-and-forth about technical or instructional issues that may arise. Eventually both departments create a series of either videos or step-sets highlighting the areas of change that teachers and students should be aware of.

When the kinks have been worked out and tested on a few pilot machines, the message to all staff and students to update goes out, along with a handy guide of what new features they might find most compelling. End users discover the new features and how to update properly, and, with the exception of a few user errors, the entire updating process goes off without a hitch. Without this communication and collaboration, a change can take place and completely crash and burn.

Let's consider this scenario again, only without the collaboration between departments. In that scenario, a message goes out telling teachers and students not to update their devices. The educational technology department waits for the OK before updating or just does it on their own to see what breaks. Eventually, when the IT staff feel the operating system is stable enough, they send out a message giving the green light to update.

Staff update their devices and immediately notice some new features, so they ask the educational technologists for support on how to use them. The ed techs, having never seen the new features themselves, cannot adequately support them. In addition, many staff didn't update properly and, as a result, lose most of their important data. The phone begins to ring off the hook as angry teachers are trying to figure out how to "turn back time" and get their data back. This could have all been avoided with the proper amount of communication and collaboration with professional learning.

Parents

Parent buy-in and ownership of a mobile device initiative can play a vital role in its success. If you think about situations where a school-issued device goes home on a daily basis, that means that almost 66% of the time, the device is off-campus. In a school-issued mobile device initiative, parent support falls into one of three categories in general:

1. How to repair a damaged device.

2. How to block or restrict certain parts of the device.

3. How to troubleshoot or support the device when it is at home.

Let's take each of the above and dissect the parent point of view and also how to best support them.

How to Repair a Damaged Device

Damage and accidents will happen. If you are sitting at a table with 10 friends and you ask them all to take out their cell phones and place them face-up on the table, you'll likely see at least one with a cracked screen. With increased mobility comes increased risk of damage. Part of the reason why we offer optional insurance (gone over in greater detail in Chapter 6) is to help parents with the high cost of repairs and replacement.

Even though we communicate this to parents ahead of time, some will opt out. Those who do opt to use the insurance can still be left frustrated when their student breaks the school-issued device. Sometimes there is a thought that if the district hadn't handed their child an expensive device, they wouldn't have to pay for this. Like everything else, communicating clearly what is considered covered under warranty (like factory glitches) versus wear and tear (like dings, dents, and scratches) versus careless or accidental damage (like broken keys or screens) is important. When a device is damaged, there needs to be an easy way for parents to see how much they will owe for the repairs. None of this should be a surprise to them. Communicating that early and often will help ease the mind of the frustrated parent in the long run.

How to Block or Restrict Certain Parts of the Device

Even with a high level of restrictions placed on a device, some families will feel the need to further restrict a school-issued device. In most of these situations, try to listen to what the parent wants and why they want it. Adding further restrictions on top of the global ones in place can make learning challenging for the student. In extreme cases, I find it best to bring in the campus administration as well to sit down with the parents and talk about the importance of having certain parts open to teach students self-restraint while also listening and adjusting based on the concerns of the parents.

As a general rule of thumb, try to not create a lot of one-off devices with varieties of restrictions. If you have a way to manage the devices globally, you could create an additional more restrictive profile to place those devices in rather than just make individual adjustments. This will help with support of the device down the road, and when the parents feel like their child is responsible enough, it makes it easier to switch them back to the global profile of restrictions.

How to Troubleshoot or Support the Device at Home

By going forward with a mobile device initiative, whether school-issued or BYOD, the school district is saying that it supports learning anytime and anywhere. This means you also need to be prepared for issues to arise at home when a student can't access a particular resource or website. This can be very challenging to support when every home environment likely has a different internet service provider (ISP) and different bandwidth constraints.

Having a resource page where parents can go for support even after hours helps alleviate much of the frustrations when something isn't working. (Ours is here: mrhook.it/parents.) However, know that a resource page shouldn't be seen as "doing enough" to support parents at home. Working with teachers and instructional coaches on best practices for home use will create a greater number of resources to be contacted in the event something goes awry or won't work on a home network. Collaborating with campus and district administration on hosting some parent nights to hear and discuss common issues also helps open up communication between technology departments and the community. Holding some sort of common "office hours" over the summer (if you plan to let students take the device home) also will help direct them to a time to come in for questions or repairs rather than having a constant barrage of emails and phone calls on top of your normal duties.

These little actions, while they take up a chunk of time, can go a long way in making the community at large feel supported in a mobile device initiative.

CHAPTER 10

REFLECT, REFINE, AND ADAPT

A successful technology department is one that finds the happy medium between supporting current initiatives, helping staff with outages, and keeping an eye on the ever-changing landscape of the educational technology future. I have highlighted ways to help with each of these concepts in this book, but one I haven't mentioned is when and how to take time to reflect and improve your department over time.

A lot of times in the middle of a mobile device initiative, you can feel like a captain on a burning ship. You spend most of your time putting out fires or plugging holes to keep the ship afloat, so much so that you don't ever have time to steer the ship. Tending to fires and holes exclusively is a great way to have your ship crash in the end.

So how do you do it all? How do you maintain your current systems and still keep abreast of the goals and vision of the district going forward? When is there ever truly such a thing as down time?

The truth is, a leader of IT who successfully balances life and work within their department will have less burnout and greater job satisfaction. As I've mentioned before, that can be challenging when every phone call your department receives is usually one of trouble or panic. Having systems and schedules in place that create that balance are important. It's equally important to take time to reflect and see where inefficiencies may exist to add to that stress.

Creating a Feedback System

Opening yourself up to feedback can be an extremely stressful thing. As a teacher, I used to get extremely nervous the night before my "formal observation," otherwise known as the "dog and pony show." I would try to visualize myself in the classroom and rehearse with my students so that their reactions would seem genuine and not at all rehearsed—if that makes sense.

I remember early in my teaching career, I decided to scrap what I thought was the "safe lesson" and try to push the envelope a little bit. I created an interactive lesson using the four desktop computers in my room and my television that projected what the kids could see. I created a video to "hook" the kids into the week-long project then outlined all the things I expected my room full of 6-year-olds to accomplish during the project. Each of them would have time on the computer throughout the week to create their own interactive presentation around a certain animal. I thought it was great project and great teaching moment in my life, and how great to have it observed formally!

Unfortunately, when my observing administrator pulled me into her office afterwards, she gave me a bad review. She said that while the kids and myself seemed enthusiastic toward the project, it was all too much. I was asking too much of myself and my kids and would probably be better off doing something a little more basic to accomplish the learning objective. She even mentioned that I might want to consider something other than teaching.

This feedback left me devastated—partly because I felt like the administrator had no real clue what I was trying to accomplish, and partly because I took a risk and it crashed and burned. The truth is, she really had no clue, because she only had one opportunity to observe me in the entire year. If I had invited her in early in the year she would have seen how I was slowly building the computer skills of these students throughout the year so this wouldn't be as overwhelming as she thought. Also, as an administrator who used to be in a first grade classroom, she had never thought of or had the resources to create such an activity. Technology had changed since her time in the classroom.

There are two lessons for an IT administrator to learn from this. One is that gathering feedback and communicating with others should be a fairly constant process. This can be done either by formal feedback forms or by simply walking around campuses and being present and visible so that staff can ask for questions or support.

The other is never losing the perspective of the changes in the classroom and how much the actions of the IT department affect learning. One of the things I've mentioned in a couple of the previous books in this series is my eye-opening reflection on being a student for a day (mrhook.it/s4ad and Figure 10.1). I was extremely proud of our 1:1 program, but going into multiple classrooms as a student showed me the areas where we were succeeding and the areas where we were still lacking.

Having that knowledge admittedly put a dent in my pride, as I'd assumed that everything was running perfectly in every classroom. This day as a student showed me that we still had a lot of work to do both technically (some of the devices weren't working) and instructionally (some teachers still didn't see the value in using them). I could do two things with that feedback. I could ignore it or take action on it. Any leader worth their salt will always choose the latter over the former.

Figure 10.1 My day as a high school student.

Improving Practice and Awareness of Trends

In a constantly evolving space, it is important for IT departments to maintain the latest certifications, but also have some time for professional development and growth themselves. This can come in the form of webinars on the latest trends or attending a conference that integrates best practices of learning with technology. Keeping this "lifelong learner" mindset in a department tells your staff that you value learning and growth as much as maintenance and support of existing technology.

One thing that I would highly recommend is attending conferences with other leaders and instructional staff so that all are on the same page with those latest trends and can have a common language of understanding. I know of many an IT department that would get frustrated after teachers attended a conference like ISTE (iste.org) because they would come back all fired up about a new idea or tool and want to put it into practice. The easiest solutions would be to simply say no or do not allow staff to attend these events, but in reality, their excitement and engagement in a new way of using technology for learning is what your department should be all about.

Although time away from the district can always be a challenge, try and find time to attend these same events with staff. Not only will you improve your professional learning, you'll have a greater understanding of where they are coming from with a certain tool or program that has them excited.

Creating a Network

I've mentioned this in all six books, and it applies with equal importance here. You can't grow and improve in isolation. Too many times I see a technology person who spends his or her time locked in a closet somewhere toiling away over computer parts while muttering under their breath about how much they just wish people wouldn't "mess with stuff."

Depending on the size of your district, you may be the only person who does what you do. Seeking out others in the field is imperative to share ideas and troubleshooting when issues arise. I was lucky enough to learn this early on in our mobile device initiative. I sent out messages on our TEC-SIG community listserv before we even got started to see who else had embarked on this challenge. I reached out on Twitter asking for anyone who had advice or resources that they would be willing to share.

At one point, I spoke via Skype to a person in Canada and another in Argentina who had both had some experience with mobile learning. Their words of advice greatly helped me understand the challenges that I might expect to face and plan accordingly. Although we still made many mistakes (see my Chapter 2 in every book), I feel that these mistakes were easier to overcome because we avoided the *big* ones.

This book was written to give you access to those best practices and things to avoid. However, don't think for a second that reading this book series will automatically make your mobile device initiative a smashing success.

It takes time.

It takes effort.

It takes constant communication.

It takes a mindset of constant learning and improvement.

We have never been completely satisfied with our program, and in some ways, I think that's a good thing. Everyone has areas to grow and improve. Technology is always changing, and that gives us even more opportunities to grow and improve. Use your network and resources to help with that improvement, but also take time to reflect on how far you've come.

Leading a mobile device initiative is the most challenging thing you will ever attempt in education. It is also the most rewarding. Remember that.

REFERENCES

Eanes ISD. (2016a). Best Practices for School-Issued iPad Usage. Retrieved from http://www.eanesisd.net/leap/students/bestpractices

Eanes ISD. (2016b). Digital Learning Task Force. Retrieved from http://www.eanesisd.net/taskforce/dltf

Eanes ISD. (2014). Hill Country Middle School iPad Oath as created by Lisa Johnson. Retrieved from http://www.techlearning.com/portals/0/CarlHooker_devices_iPadOath.pdf

Eanes ISD. (2016c). iPad Protection Plans. Retrieved from http://www.eanesisd.net/leap/plans

Eanes ISD. (2016d). LEAP Initiative: Learning and Engaging through Access and Personalization. Retrieved from https://eanesisd.net/leap

Eanes ISD. (2016e). LEAP Initiative - For Parents. Retrieved from http://eanesisd.net/leap/parents

Eanes ISD. (2015). Responsible Use Guidelines (2015) Retrieved from http://www.eanesisd.net/students-and-parents/enrollment/docs/WHS-RUG

Johnson, L. (2013). I Declare an….iPad Oath. Retrieved from https://techchef4u.com/2013/08/ipad-oath/

Madda, M. (2016). Alan November on the '$1000 Pencil' and Why Edtech Companies Aren't Pushing the Envelope. Retrieved from https://www.edsurge.com/news/2016-08-15-alan-november-on-the-1000-pencil-and-why-edtech-companies-aren-t-pushing-the-envelope

Sinek, S. (2009). How Great Leaders Inspire Action [TED Talk]. Retrieved from http://www.ted.com/talks/simon_sinek_how_great_leaders_inspire_action?language=en

ISTE STANDARDS

The ISTE Standards for Administrators (ISTE Standards·A)

All school administrators should be prepared to meet the following standards and performance indicators.

1. **Visionary Leadership**

   Administrators inspire and lead development and implementation of a shared vision for comprehensive integration of technology to promote excellence and support transformation throughout the organization. Administrators:

   a. Inspire and facilitate among all stakeholders a shared vision of purposeful change that maximizes use of digital age resources to meet and exceed learning goals, support effective instructional practice and maximize performance of district and school leaders.

   b. Engage in an ongoing process to develop, implement and communicate technology-infused strategic plans aligned with a shared vision.

   c. Advocate on local, state and national levels for policies, programs and funding to support implementation of a technology-infused vision and strategic plan.

2. **Digital Age Learning Culture**

Administrators create, promote and sustain a dynamic, digital age learning culture that provides a rigorous, relevant and engaging education for all students. Administrators:

   a. Ensure instructional innovation focused on continuous improvement of digital age learning.

   b. Model and promote the frequent and effective use of technology for learning.

   c. Provide learner-centered environments equipped with technology and learning resources to meet the individual, diverse needs of all learners.

   d. Ensure effective practice in the study of technology and its infusion across the curriculum.

   e. Promote and participate in local, national and global learning communities that stimulate innovation, creativity and digital age collaboration.

3. **Excellence in Professional Practice**

Administrators promote an environment of professional learning and innovation that empowers educators to enhance student learning through the infusion of contemporary technologies and digital resources. Administrators:

   a. Allocate time, resources and access to ensure ongoing professional growth in technology fluency and integration.

   b. Facilitate and participate in learning communities that stimulate, nurture and support administrators, faculty and staff in the study and use of technology.

   c. Promote and model effective communication and collaboration among stakeholders using digital age tools.

d. Stay abreast of educational research and emerging trends regarding effective use of technology and encourage evaluation of new technologies for their potential to improve student learning.

4. Systemic Improvement

Administrators provide digital age leadership and management to continuously improve the organization through the effective use of information and technology resources. Administrators:

a. Lead purposeful change to maximize the achievement of learning goals through the appropriate use of technology and media-rich resources.

b. Collaborate to establish metrics, collect and analyze data, interpret results and share findings to improve staff performance and student learning.

c. Recruit and retain highly competent personnel who use technology creatively and proficiently to advance academic and operational goals.

d. Establish and leverage strategic partnerships to support systemic improvement.

e. Establish and maintain a robust infrastructure for technology including integrated, interoperable technology systems to support management, operations, teaching and learning.

5. Digital Citizenship

Administrators model and facilitate understanding of social, ethical and legal issues and responsibilities related to an evolving digital culture. Administrators:

a. Ensure equitable access to appropriate digital tools and resources to meet the needs of all learners.

b. Promote, model and establish policies for safe, legal and ethical use of digital information and technology.

c. Promote and model responsible social interactions related to the use of technology and information.

d. Model and facilitate the development of a shared cultural understanding and involvement in global issues through the use of contemporary communication and collaboration tools.

© 2012 International Society for Technology in Education (ISTE), iste.org. All rights reserved.